Freedom From
Financial
Funk

CHARLIE + COUANN

I PRAY THAT GOD WILL
USE THIS BOOK AND BLESS YOU
RICHLY.

Freedom From
Financial
Funk

How to Survive and Even Thrive
In Today's Economy

Dean Stein

Table of Contents

Chapter 1:   The Early Years: A Success Story 3

Chapter 2:   Defining Moment #1. 13

Chapter 3:   Back on the Entrepreneurial Track – Crash #1 . . 19

Chapter 4:   Defining Moment #2. 35

Chapter 5:   Movin' on Up 49

Chapter 6:   Self Employment Revisited – Crash #2 63

Chapter 7:   Defining Moment #3. 77

Chapter 8:   Success is Born 83

Chapter 9:   Defining Moment #4. 89

Chapter 10:   Another Successful Business is Born 97

Chapter 11:   Crash #3 The Economy 107

Chapter 12:   The Infamous "Joseph Calling" 119

Chapter 13:   10 Attitudes For Doing
               Business Supernaturally. 125

Chapter 14:   Dos and Don'ts Concerning Money 131

Chapter 15:   Financial Principles For Debt, Investing,
               & Spending 135

Chapter 16:   Time: A Blessing or a Curse 147

Chapter 17:   Setting Goals 153

Chapter 18:   The Size of a Butter Patty 159

Chapter 19:   The Pond 165

Chapter 20:   Let's Talk Real Estate 169

Chapter 21:   Three Ways Rental Real Estate
              Makes You Money 173

Chapter 22:   Six Steps to Determine if a Property is
              a Good Investment. 177

Chapter 23:   A Few Closing Thoughts on Real Estate 185

Chapter 24:   In Conclusion 189

              Bibliography. 193

Dedication

I dedicate this book to Jenny, my wife of 32 years, and our 5 unbelievably fantastic children, Daniel, David, Andrew Lizzie and Chris. To my three beautiful daughters-in-law, Sarah, Tracey and Pamela, and my 9 precious grandchildren, Kirra, Eli, Blake, Paige, Sophie, Bella, Josiah, Abi and the one on the way.

Some say only rich men should write business books and, thanks to my family,
I am the richest man I know.

Introduction

Why would anyone want to read my book? I am not a multi-millionaire. I don't have prestigious awards and certificates decorating the walls of my Wall Street office. Nor do I frequently receive invitations to speak at conferences. So why read my book? Or better yet, why write a book in the first place?

The answer is simple; I am just like you. I'm an average Joe. I wasn't born with a silver spoon in my mouth. I'm probably less educated than the average person reading this book and I didn't have a father to mentor me growing up. I started out with nothing. For most of the world, my beginning would determine my end, but not here, not for you. You and I have a unique opportunity. Whether we start at the bottom or somewhere along the way, we have all the resources to make a better economical future for our families and ourselves. The first half of my qualification to write this book is this; I am one of you.

On the other hand, to date I have started seven different businesses, the first when I was just eight years old. I own millions of dollars in real estate investments. In spite of my lack of education (a fake high school diploma), in the last two decades I have made millions of dollars and generated over half a billion dollars in loans for my clients. More importantly, however, I have lost everything I own, twice, and earned it all back again, and more. When the economic earthquake hit in 2008, my business completely dried up for six months. I went from the third quarter of 2008 to the second quarter of 2009 with zero income. It was then that, once again, I put the principles to work that I will cover in this book. They have caused me to survive, and even thrive, in a post-2008 economy.

I have had four defining moments in my life and survived three financial crashes. While my experiences and accomplishments may be enough to qualify me to write this book, the truth is, all my knowledge and success comes from the fact that I have learned two things:

- What the word of G-d, laid out through scripture, says about business

- How to hear and follow the voice of the Lord in business decisions

In these unprecedented economic times, the experiences I have endured, successes and failures, can help guide you through to the other side, and cause you to be financially better off at the end.

This book is divided into two sections:

My Story:

As I go through the story of my life from a business perspective, you will most likely relate to the successes I have had, as well as the failures I have experienced.

These lessons will guide you in learning how to survive, and even thrive, in today's economy.

Let's get Practical:

This section will be an action plan outlining practical steps to make it through an economic downturn such as we have faced following 2008. Furthermore, I will identify and lay out opportunities to build and increase your personal wealth from a practical standpoint.

It is my sincere hope that you will gain abundantly more than I have, by learning from the journey I have been so privileged to endure.

Part One
My Story

Chapter One
The Early Years: A Success Story

*Having graduated high school and working
at the local grocery store as a bagger, I figured
my next step was rock-stardom.*

Growing up Poor:

I grew up in a poor family. Dad was a struggling entrepreneur with a great deal more intelligence than success. Money and things were something other people had.

I would often ask my mother, "Has anyone in the family ever made it big?" On one such occasion, she went to the closet and pulled out an old 45 record. If memory serves me correctly, on one side of the Epic Records 45 was a song titled, "Woman without Love," that was her favorite song. On the other side was "Evil Woman." The recording came from an aspiring performer, T. D. Valentine. His mother and my grandmother were sisters. He married the founder of ABC records' daughter and was doing quite well for himself. T. D. Valentine goes by his real name now, former head of Sony Music and current performing philanthropist, Tommy Mottola, who at one time was married to Mariah Carey. To this day I have never met Tommy, but as a child he was a ray of hope for me. I would think to myself, *if just one person in my family can make it, someday, I could make it.* Even as a young adult I never let go of that thought, that hope.

My mother converted from Catholicism to Judaism and married my father, a Romanian Jew. They had three children, of which I am the middle child and only son.

As a boy, I remember the Good Humor truck coming down Jefferson Blvd in Staten Island. All three of us children would run up to my mother, each wanting a dime for ice cream. She would go to her oversized pocketbook and pull out a small change purse. Sometimes there were three dimes for her to hand out, other times there was that, all-too-often look of disappointment on her face as she closed the purse and said, "Not today."

The car I remember liking the most was the grey station wagon. I loved this car, because, from where I sat in the back seat, I could look down and see the road going by under my feet. The car's floorboards were rusted clear through.

I never really knew I was so poor (even though I hated wearing hand-me-down corduroys) due to the fact that we never went hungry and we were never dirty.

My father was an entrepreneur. He had many different businesses, including a restaurant, an epicurean shop that sold chocolate covered ants, and a distributorship for Five and Dime stores called Lor-Dee, named after my sister Lori and myself. He planned to change the name to Lor-Dee-Mar when my sister, Marcie was born, but never got around to it.

He passed away in 1966; I was just five years old. My father was the youngest of 7 children. Benny, Simon, Max, Rose, Pepi, Clara and Jonas, along with their mother Leah, left Romania in 1931. They came to America, arrived at Ellis Island, and from there it gets a little fuzzy. I know at some point after moving to NY, my father lived in Israel for three years.

It makes me sad to think that, if my father had lived just one more year, almost to the day, he would have seen our people restored to the land of Jerusalem after 2,000 years.

His last business before he died was the distributorship. As a result, he left our basement full of Five and Dime products. Among the merchandise were blue and pink bottles of blowing bubbles, pencils with oversized erasers, composition books and hologram key chains.

I remember running up the basement stairs with a hologram key chain featuring the Virgin Mary. When moved, the last supper appeared on the surface. I was furious at my father. Yelling, I asked my mother why Dad would sell this Jesus stuff. She said, "If he could make a buck, he would make a buck."

I attended the Jewish Foundation School on Staten Island for five years, kindergarten through fourth grade. Half the day we learned to read and write Hebrew and the history of Abraham, Isaac and Jacob. The second half was spent learning how to read and write English. How we didn't develop dyslexia having to write and read from right to left half the day, and left to right the other half is a mystery to me.

I was a terrible student and remember each year hearing my mother argue they shouldn't hold me back because I had such a high IQ. She would insist they give me an IQ test to pass me. Although I never did see my scores, they always would test me and I would always move to the next grade.

Entering the work force:

Since my mother never had money to spare, I followed in dad's footsteps, almost by default. I began my first business at the age of eight. I was too young for a paper route, so I made a deal. I negotiated with the kid who ran the route in my neighborhood. I would run papers to x amount of houses for so much money. Going door-to-door on my bicycle gave me an idea for my next move.

I put a basket on my Stingray bicycle built from parts I found in the woods (remember, this was 1969 and there were plenty of woods in Staten Island). I loaded it up with my father's old merchandise from the basement and a cigar box to store the large quantities of money I would be making. Each time I sold a bottle of blowing bubbles I made ten cents. Never again did I need to ask mom for Good Humor ice cream money. I found my niche delivering newspapers and selling merchandise door to door. My lucrative new business, however, was about to change.

The only vacation our family ever went on was to a little

town in upstate NY in the Alleghany foothills called Wellsville, New York. We stayed for 2 weeks at a friend's house.

Other than the house, there was nothing else. There was hardly a neighbor in site and absolutely nothing to do. I was used to NYC and went on vacation to a field. Don't take this the wrong way. The area was absolutely beautiful with its lush fields, thick woods and scenic dairy farms. It was just such a drastic difference from Staten Island.

In 1973 we moved to Andover, New York, the neighboring town to our luxurious vacation spot. My mother said it was cheaper to live there and we would have a better life. The only problem was my business was now in jeopardy. The closest neighbor was a quarter mile up the road. Not wanting to retire at the young age of 12, I took what I had learned and ran with it.

The nearest neighbor just happened to be a dairy farm. I went to work each day after school and on the weekends, milking cows and shoveling manure. After one month I received my first paycheck; $15.00. They must have seen me coming. The next month they doubled my pay; $30.00. Apparently they were smart businessmen and didn't want to lose their talented farm hand. With $45.00 in my pocket I found my first major investment—I bought a calf. There was an old barn across the street from our house. The owner informed me there was no water or electricity but I was welcome to use it.

I worked the next month for the $30 cash, plus all the hay, straw and McNess Calf Starter (livestock formula) I needed. Every day, before and after school, I would carry water and feed to the barn and feed my calf. Three months later I took the calf to market and made $120. With this new business plan, I was turning a calf a quarter, in addition to my whopping $30/month salary. I was now making $210 every three months. Enter the world of high finance.

I named my first calf Rickets, the second Scurvy and the third Beriberi. My mother was a little concerned seeing my animals named after diseases, so I changed to naming them all derivatives of drop. Gum Drop, Rain Drop, Tear Drop... you get the drift.

When my life and ability to make money changed based on my mother's decision to move, I could have thought, *without a neighborhood, there's no way to earn money. I'll just waste my time playing video games.* Lucky for me, had video games been invented, we wouldn't have been able to afford them. However, since my mother had no means of giving me the things I wanted, I was forced to figure out how to earn money. This is a blessing in my life, not a curse. All too often, we as parents shortchange our children. Never wanting to say no, we give them the "things" they would otherwise gladly learn how to achieve on their own.

A successful jewelry store owner once told me a piece of his story. He was graduating from selling jewelry out of the trunk of his car to his first storefront. He came up a thousand dollars short for rent one month and went to his father for help. His father agreed to help. After visiting for the evening, just before leaving, he asked his father for the check. To his surprise, his dad said he never agreed to give him a check. The father informed his young entrepreneurial son that the best way he could help was to allow him to figure out a solution himself. If he knew his dad would always be there to bail him out, then he could never grow beyond his dad's wherewithal. Today, he is much more successful than his dad ever was. The student should always surpass the teacher.

At the same time I was involved in ranching my own head of cattle, I began working for other farms in the neighborhood as well. I worked at several dairy farms, a Christmas tree farm and a potato farm before I landed my first executive position flipping hamburgers at McDonalds.

As a 16-year-old working at McDonalds, I always picked up my friends' hours when they didn't want them. I remember thinking to myself, "Don't they want the money?" It never occurred to me that parents gave their kids money. I didn't have a choice; I would have had nothing if I didn't work. The result was that, at the age of 16, I had already purchased a 1963 Triumph TR4 and a 1969 Mustang. I paid for my own tires, maintenance, insurance and gas, (52 cents/gallon). Before graduating high school, I also had a 1969 Impala, a 1970 Malibu Chevelle, a Ford Custom and a customized Ford van with the Rolling Stones tongue painted on the back doors. Not bad for a poor kid. Now, don't get me wrong, these cars were clunkers. The Mustang for example was two-tone, blue and primer grey. But I was one of the few kids in 10th grade with my own car.

Education, however, was still not my strong point. To make

matters worse, I smoked my first joint and was hooked on the party life at the age of 14. I would smoke before school, during lunch, after school and at night. In between classes I snorted whatever was available. When I turned 16, I began drinking on a regular basis. Life was an unending party, and here came my demise. My entrepreneurial spirit died. I always worked because I needed money, only now, it was money to keep up my car and buy more drugs. The only ambition I had left was to be a rock star. The fact that I did not sing or play an instrument was never a deterrent. I had long hair, I looked cool and I loved Aerosmith— what else did I need?

By the time I was a senior in high school I had been thrown out of most classes and only went to school when I felt like seeing some friends. Mom was called in once again, and informed that there was no way the school could graduate me. I didn't have enough days by law and not enough credits. My mother convinced them that keeping me would only mean heartache; it would be in everyone's best interest to give me a diploma. They did.

As a graduate working at the local grocery store as a bagger, I figured my next step was rock-stardom. The grocery store manager, noticing my willingness to take extra hours, sat me down. He presented me with a life question, "What are your plans?" That was an easy one—"I'm going to be a rock star."

He was gracious. He asked me if I wanted to get a raise and start working full time, learning to be a meat cutter for $3.65 an hour, just until my music career was realized. Since my cousin, Tommy had not yet called, I accepted the offer.

Lessóns Learned

- For those who desire to be successful, the glass always needs to be half full. The old saying, when life gives you lemons make lemonade needs to be a knee-jerk reaction if you are going to overcome the obstacles life will throw at you.

- A person has no say in where they are born or what socio-economic situation they are born into. Our life choices are what take us to our destinies, not the cards that life deals us.

- If a person wants an excuse to be lazy, poor, or live off the government, most of us do not have to look far. On the other hand, successful people take those very same "excuses," and use them as motivating devices to prove to themselves and the world that they can make it.

- We live in the land of "opportunity," not the land of "entitlement." Our Declaration of Independence says all men are created equal. However, all men do not stay equal. Some take that freedom and make something of it; others take that same freedom and do nothing with it. It is not the government's or anybody else's job to "keep" all men equal. It is the individual's job to make the most of his life with what he has been given.

Chapter Two
Defining Moment #1

I kept thinking to myself, this guy (Jesus) knows
what He is supposed to do to fulfill scripture, so
He does it, and these fools fall for it.

Defining Moment #1

It didn't take long to realize I wasn't cut out for cutting meat. I guess you could say I didn't make the cut. (A little humor, very little). I have always hated cold weather and the meat room was always cold.

After high school, my two best friends moved to Louisiana and were making $7 an hour as laborers building an oil refinery.

They came back for a visit and invited me to return with them. I told my mother I was leaving and left that morning, starting a 1000 plus mile journey from Andover, New York to Sulfur, Louisiana, just outside Lake Charles.

Not long after arriving, I went to a Pizza Hut for dinner. Little did I know, that day would change the direction of my life forever—literally for eternity.

The waitress was cute, so I asked her out. She said she would go out with me but, I needed to know she was a Christian. Being willing to take risks, I said, "Oh good, I am too."

After our date we walked in a K-mart to buy something and, without thinking twice, I lit up a joint. Somehow she knew right away that I was not a Christian.

By this time I had secured the position of a guard at a lay down yard. My sole responsibility was to keep a record of truck arrivals and departures so as to assure the drivers didn't make any unnecessary detours. I recorded fictitious times if the drivers brought me beer or pot. I was making $8.15 an hour now and working four, 10-hour days. This freed me up to have three-day weekends to party.

One day, the girl from Pizza Hut showed up at my work with the Children's Living Bible. She said since I didn't really do anything all day long but get high, I should read this Bible. I thought, "If Jesus was a Jew, he couldn't be all that bad," so I began to read. Due to the fact that I had never read a single book before, this particular version of the Bible was perfect for me to understand.

There were a few other reasons that I decided to read that book.

When I was 14 years old, just prior to the time I smoked my first joint, I had a dream. I was standing on a tall tower with Roman soldiers trying to throw me off. The tower was very high and I was looking down on clouds. I started yelling for help when Jesus came up to me, walking on the air, and said, "Unless you believe in Me, I can not help you." I yelled at him and told him

I would never believe in him. He said "Then my hands are tied." He put them behind his back and the soldiers threw me off. As I was falling through the air, I yelled, "Jesus, I believe in you." In an instant, I was back on the tower, the soldiers were gone and it was just Jesus and me. I looked at him with hate filled eyes, pointed my finger in his face, and yelled, "I'll never believe in you, you jerk!" I woke up. From that day on I had a real fear of death.

Ironically, a week or so prior to receiving the Bible, I was driving over the Lake Charles Bridge in my 1973, 350 Chevelle, listening to my 8 track of Foreigner's song, "Blinded by Science". The words went something like this:

> *I'm worried about the world that we live in and all this confusion. I wonder where this madness is leading, or if we're here for no reason. Is this a road going nowhere, or is someone leading us somewhere? Blinded science, I'm on the run.*

I had listened to this song a hundred times. For some reason, this time, I had the same questions the lyrics asked. You see, I had achieved all that I wanted in life. Granted, at this point the bar wasn't set too high. But I had a cool car with a fast engine, a girl friend, I was making more money than I had ever made before and was out on my own. My hair was long and my ear was pierced. I had all the drugs I wanted (only rock stardom had eluded me), and yet, I was not fulfilled.

So here I am now in my little guard shack at work reading

the Bible, I kept thinking to myself, *this guy knows what He is supposed to do to fulfill scripture, so He does it, and these fools fall for it.* It wasn't until I read the part about not breaking his bones. What I didn't know then, but know now, is that to be the promised Messiah, he had to be crucified, but without any of his bones being broken. This was key to fulfilling the scriptures and it was something he had no control over. For some reason, with tears rolling down my face, I stood up over the Bible and began shouting, "Break His bones, prove He's not the Messiah." And then, right then, for reasons at the time I couldn't understand, I believed He was the Jewish Messiah.

What a relief I felt. I am Jewish, so I was going to heaven anyway. Now I believe that Jesus is the Messiah. I have this thing covered.

I began telling my friends they should get right with Jesus like I did. One night, while getting drunk and high, I was sharing Jesus with a friend. He asked why I was going to Heaven with a beer in one hand and a joint in the other, while he was going to Hell?

I thought for a minute and said, "Rick, you're right. I am going to quit these drugs for G-d." The next morning I woke up and said, "Today, I quit." By noon I was stoned. The next day, I woke up and said, "Today, I quit." By noon I was stoned. This went on for four months. I could stop getting drunk, I could even stop the harder drugs, but I could not stop smoking pot. As soon as I smoked a joint, I figured I was high anyways and then did harder stuff, followed by heavy drinking.

One evening, I took Miss Pizza Hut to dinner and ordered

a bottle of wine. Like a gentleman, I offered, but she refused. I drank the bottle myself. Drunk on the drive back, I dropped her off, went home, and walked into my house where a huge party was taking place. I yelled, "I'm never going out with those #$%@^&* Christians again."

At three in the morning, after partying hard all night, I crawled on my hands and knees to my bed. I lay there and cried out to Jesus. I told him I simply couldn't do it; I couldn't quit. I told him I didn't care what he did with my life; he could even make me a preacher (the worst thing I could think of that he would do). Immediately, I was sober and slept like a baby.

The next morning I woke up and came out of my bedroom. One of my friends handed me a joint. It was good Columbian Gold. I could smell how good it was. I handed the joint back to him and said, "I quit." He laughed, "Dean, you quit every day, quit tomorrow, this stuff is good." I told him that for four months I had been trying to quit for the Lord, but last night I gave Him my life and He just took the desire away from me.

For the next several months I dove into the word of G-d and became a sponge. I would share Jesus with people, then run back to my pastor and ask him if what I said was true. He always opened the Bible to show me where it was written. I was learning how to hear and follow the voice of the Lord.

I was never the same. It wasn't long before I was heading back to New York to tell my family what happened to me.

While my mother was the hardest to convince, she just

could not deny the change in my life and ended up giving her life to the Lord as well. The real shocker was when I arrived home; the Lord had already met my older sister.

G-d was at work in my life and was laying out a path for me to follow.

Lessons Learned

- You can spend your whole life destroying what you have, wasting your time and talents. In one second, when exposed to the Truth, your whole life and destiny can be brought into focus.

- There is a defining moment in every person's life. Sometimes that moment is anti-climactic, but a defining moment none-the-less. If we embrace, rather than reject it, it will serve to guide us through the rest of our journey.

Chapter Three
Back on the Entrepreneurial Track - Crash #1

We opened and ran four stores with no budget,
no business plan, no inventory records and no books.

Learning to Sell

As I mentioned in chapter one, when I started smoking pot, my entrepreneurial spirit died. Well, it didn't take long for it to come back once I turned my life around. After returning to New York, I fell in love, got married and had the first of our five children. A year later we bought our first house. I needed to make money.

The only job I could land was at the same supermarket I worked at for while in high school. There I was, back at the Giant Food Mart, working the night shift. My responsibilities amounted to stocking shelves, making $110 a week. I knew there had to be more.

Having no education, however, I didn't know what I could

do. I prayed, asking G-d what I should do. The paper advertised a job saying I could earn $250 a week. My wife, Jenny and I went to the meeting.

A man stood up and said, "My name is Fred Voss and I'm with Consolidated Foods." My wife blurted out, "Oh good, I was afraid this was vacuum cleaner sales." He paused, and then explained that Consolidated Foods owns Electrolux.

At the end of the meeting I asked him if he really thought I could make $250 a week in commissions. "I'm positive you can," he replied. I asked him, if he was so positive, why didn't he guarantee me the $250 a week? He made me a deal. He would guarantee it for three months. At the end of the three months, if I wasn't making it on my own, we could go our separate ways.

However, my sales abilities did not start out very well. I thought I was putting on these amazing presentations during my sales pitches, and yet, somehow, I couldn't close a deal. I decided to take an old pro along with me, someone who had made his living selling these machines for nearly 20 years. After putting on a great presentation and leaving the house without a sale, I turned to him and asked what I was doing wrong. "Didn't I put on a good presentation and cover all the bases?" I got a nice pat on the back. He said he watched me talk myself right into the sale, and then talk myself right out of the sale. "Shut up," he said, "you talk way too much." *Story of my life,* I thought. I took his advice and began making sales. By the time the three months were up, I was making between $250 and $300 a week going door to door as a vacuum cleaner salesman.

I would get paid on each machine I sold, plus extra commissions on things like bags and accessories. On the other hand, if a person returned their machine within a certain time period, I would have that commission deducted from my pay. I was talking to my wife's Uncle Pete about the situation since he was a successful salesman. He told me, *a real key to selling was to ask the customer before leaving the house what is their reason for buying the product. In doing so, you solidify in their minds the reason and they don't start to question their decision after you leave.*

I began doing this each time I made a sale and had very few people change their minds. One time, however, I remember selling a machine to a young girl. When I asked why she decided to purchase the vacuum for her tiny little apartment, she said it was because I was cute. Guess who turned in their machine a few days later?

Seeing I could sell, a friend of mine asked if I would like to sell insurance for Prudential. I prayed and felt I had peace from the Lord. So I went for it. Unfortunately, this is where my reproach for academia came back to bite me. I didn't understand the material. I couldn't retain the information I was studying. I knew I would fail the test and not get my insurance license. In defeat, I called my friend and told him I couldn't take the test. He asked if it was still true that I believed the Lord told me to go for this. I said yes. He then asked why I didn't believe the Lord would get me through it if it were, in fact, G-d who wanted me to do it? This man didn't even believe in Messiah at the time. I then asked the Lord to help me retain the information. Almost immediately I began understanding the content. I not only passed the life and health test, but also later passed the property and casualty exam and obtained that license as well.

I worked at Prudential successfully for 2 years—but my real desire was to own my own business.

Maybe this desire came from the fact that my father always owned his own businesses. Perhaps it was because of my early days with my first business in door-to-door sales on my bicycle, or perhaps it was just what the plan and destiny was for my life.

Crash #1

The year was 1984, my brother-in-law had just returned from Michigan where he was running a home improvement business. At the time, I was selling water purification machines. One day I asked the owner of the company if our system took Fluoride out of the water. He asked if my customer wanted it to and I told him they did. He said, "It does." Feeling a little uneasy about his answer, I asked him what his answer would have been if they didn't. He said, "Then it doesn't." I left the company. I couldn't sell anything I didn't believe in and I no longer believed in the product.

As a result, by brother-in-law and I decided to join forces and start our own company. I sold the jobs and assisted him with the manual work. Our company was named H.I.S. Company (Home Improvement Services). We started in the spring, and by winter knew we needed to do something different if we were going to make enough money to support both our families.

We looked in the yellow pages under "carpet," bought eight rolls, rented a 1,000 Ft.^{2} storefront on Main Street and, ta-da; we were in the carpet business. Our name now stood for Home Improvement Showcase. We were proud, full of optimism; we had successfully set sail. Next stop, bankruptcy.

We ran the business and showcased the carpet from our new location on Main St. Around November of that year I purchased a waterbed for myself and fell in love. We added those to our merchandise. We pushed the carpet to one side of the store and put in seven waterbeds. We had full wave, semi wave, waveless, motionless, and even a hybrid tube bed. We put a bed in the front window on Dixie Cups to show that the beds weight was evenly distributed and could be set up on the second floor of a house. We had different headboards, different mattresses and different pedestals on each bed to display as much product in as small an area as possible. We sold 117 waterbeds in just over a month.

I was now a skilled sales person and loving it. I remember listening to one of our sales people work with a customer. He took his time, thoroughly educating the customer. Then I heard, "OK we'll get back with you," as they headed towards the door. I intercepted. "I couldn't help overhearing, it sounded like you wanted headboard A, mattress B and pedestal C, is that correct?" They said it was and I asked if it was fine to have it delivered and set up by Friday. They walked out with the date in their calendar. Another lesson learned; **Always ask for the sale.** You can be extremely knowledgeable about your product, you can have the best price and service in town, you can posses a charismatic personality and be unbelievably good looking, but if you don't ask for the sale, chances are good you won't get it. This is not merely a sales technique. Whether your goal is to build up X amount in savings or attain certain numbers for your business, whatever your individual goal is, you have to "ask for the sale." It is important to not just hope these goals happen, but to identify clearly what it will take to achieve them. Doing whatever you must do to see your goals become a reality is your way of "asking for the sale."

It's now July of 1985 and we've added TV's and VCR's, both Beta and VHS. By this time our store was packed with hardly room for customer and sales people to comfortably cohabit. The clothing outlet next door had just gone out of business and we decided it was time to expand.

My brother-in-law and business partner was a talented carpenter; he could do just about anything. He took out the cinderblock wall between the two stores. We then added recliners, dinettes, sofa sleepers, regular bedding and bunk beds; we had become a full-fledged furniture store.

With the larger location, we both felt it was better to sell the home improvement part of the business and focus our attention on the retail end. Two of our employees bought this division and did well with it.

Giving birth to a profit

When my wife became pregnant in 1985 with our third son, I didn't have health insurance. I made a deal with the doctor; if he delivered my baby, I would carpet his home. He liked the idea, and after my son was born, and he showed me the bill. I showed him what carpets he could choose from. He wanted a better grade carpet so I gave him an upgrade. He paid the difference and I made a nice profit on the birth of my third son. I believe Father Abraham would have been proud.

It's still 1985. H.I.S. Company's inventory has grown tremendously. We have doubled our location size, but we still aren't making enough to support ourselves. At this point we decided to open another store 45 minutes from our current location. Soon thereafter we took out our first bank loan to purchase 2 more stores from a chain that was going out of business.

One of the stores was in the same town as our existing first store, just a couple of blocks down the road, also on Main Street. The other store was about 45 minutes in the other direction. We hired a company to put the stores into a "Going out of Business Sale" for us. They brought in enormous amounts of furniture and we all made good money running the stores out of business under the old name, and then reopening them under the H.I.S. Company name.

With the new space, 4,000 and 6,000 square feet, we added dining rooms, living rooms, bedrooms, lamps, end tables, coffee tables, oriental rugs and more.

We had four locations and 2 large delivery trucks and yet we still could not make enough money. Looking back now, knowing what I know, it wasn't a lack of money; it was a lack of money management. *Money is only the answer when money is the problem.* If our government system would realize this truth and stop throwing endless dollars of our tax money to fix all our problems, our country would be in much better shape. This is something we need to learn at every level. It's just like "The size of your butter patty," which we will talk about in subsequent chapters. Proper management is applicable as an individual, as a family, as a company and as a nation.

Since we had all this activity and trucks coming with deliveries to the three different stores on different days, we were always juggling money.

I would write a check out of one checkbook from a store in one town. Before that check would clear, I would write another check to cover it from a different checkbook from a store with a different bank in another town. Before that check cleared, I would repeat the process with a third check from a third bank, and so on and so forth.

One day, while making a deposit at one of the branches, I was called into the manager's office. He asked if I knew what check kiting was. I truthfully denied. Upon his explanation, I naively said, "oh yeah, I do that." He then informed me it was not only illegal, but he could also have me arrested on the spot.

The amount of negative checks was well into the thousands by then, and no money to cover them. We ended up having a meeting with all the banks involved and developed a plan to get them all paid. Although they were great to work with, it was becoming clear; I was in way over my head.

The thing was, I had no idea of what I was doing. When the IRS finally came down on us, we counseled with an accountant. They asked to see our books, to which I replied, "I don't ever read." They thought I was being funny; I had no idea what they meant. We opened and ran four stores with no budget, no business plan, no inventory records and no books.

We made the decision to always pay our employees, even if we there was not enough money to pay ourselves. At one point we went 16 weeks without paying ourselves. Since our salary was only $350 a week, we didn't have personal cash reserves to fall back on.

Scene One: Enter Pride

Even though we were not making very much money personally, we owned several stores in different towns. I was a legend in my own mind, as the radio spokesman for all our crazy radio advertisements. Pride entered my heart.

My real focus had become success. I was consumed with the desire to be the big businessman. *Look at the house I live in, the car I drive, how many stores I have.* It hadn't dawned on me that there might be a reason, much bigger then me, for being successful.

Eventually, all of the mistakes we made, not having a budget or business plan, the problems with the IRS, and the fact that we grew too fast all caught up with us.

I ended up losing my house, my car was repossessed, I owed

money on credit cards and was in deep to both the IRS and the State of New York.

One evening, while discussing our next move over a cup of coffee, my wife Jenny and I prayed about moving to North Carolina. We had made several trips to the area for the spring and fall furniture shows. We also visited some friends that moved there from where we lived in New York. It didn't seem to matter when we went, spring or fall, we would always leave grey skies and snow in NY and arrive in NC with the sun shining with the most beautiful blue skies you have ever seen.

We asked the Lord if He was leading us to pack up and move. We both felt a peace and decided to go. I sold my share of the business to my brother-in-law in exchange for some furniture and the use of the delivery truck for the move. He tried to keep the business running with the thought that if it only had to support one family, it might have a chance. The company was too far in the red. He shut it down a little over a year later.

I arrived in North Carolina one month before my wife and children joined me. I thought I was going ahead to secure employment, find a house and get things ready. The higher reason was a much-needed lesson in priorities.

I found a small four-room house in need of a paint job 10 years prior to my arrival. I rented that house, put a couch in the dining room and, for one month I ate, sat, and slept on that one piece of furniture. I began reading my Bible again. Through His Word, the Lord spoke four things to me.

1. Everything I do, I should do for His Name sake, not my own.

2. I must decrease in my life and he must increase.

3. Whatever I do, do it all for the Glory of G-d.

4. His Word is a lamp unto my feet, a light unto my path. He will give me enough light to walk by faith, but never so much light that I could run ahead of him. Trust is always the key.

One month later, my family left our 12 room house in NY and our repossessed brand new car and moved to our little 4 room house in an old rusty car, but we were finally back together and in the center of G-d's will; and we were happy.

Starting over isn't easy. Here I was, only 27 years old, and had already lost everything. But starting over implies a fresh start. I brought to our "new start" a debt of over 100 thousand dollars, still owing countless entities, including the state of New York and the IRS.

I had nothing to fall back on. The only option I could see was bankruptcy, which I didn't believe in, but like Bob Dylan said, "When you got nothing, you got nothing to lose." I didn't see any choice in the matter. I was making $350/week working at Rhodes Furniture as a salesman.

I went to a lawyer, filled out all the paper work and was told I could go Chapter 7 on everything except what I owed the state and federal government.

On my way to the lawyer's office, the Lord spoke clearly,

"Dean, don't go bankrupt." Now, I didn't hear an audible voice, I heard it in my spirit, an impression, like if you were to hear a voice telling you not to go down that dark alleyway. I responded in an audible voice, "Lord, that can't be you. But if it is, tell me again and I won't go bankrupt." Again, I knew in my heart He was talking to me. "Lord, I only make $350 a week, how can I ever even come close to paying off this debt?" He said to trust Him and He would show Himself faithful.

I went home and told my wife what had happened and, like always, she stood by my side.

A Ray of Hope

I always believed whatever I had was a gift from the Lord and that I had a responsibility to be a good steward over it. Even though I hated washing my $600 rust bucket, the sponge always getting caught in the holes of the car, I still took care of it as if it were new. I believed that if I did, one day, I would have something nice again.

I want you to know I really hated this car. Plastic seats, broken, cracked running board molding. It was dark, dark blue with no air conditioning; it was summer, it was North Carolina, it was full of rust and I hated that car.

Never-the-less, there I was, washing the stupid thing when the Lord spoke to me out of the blue. I wasn't praying or being spiritual, or even thinking about Him and all of a sudden I heard, "After you pay off the IRS and the state of New York, and all your other bills, I want you to pay back the church for the money they lost on their deposit."

The church I attended in New York was in the process of building a new location. They put a deposit on some carpet for the new building. The completion was delayed and by the time they were ready for the carpet, H.I.S. Company was out of business. I was never so excited in my life. I realized G-d was telling me that somehow, some way, I was going to be able to pay off all the debt.

H.I.S. Company was a legal partnership. That meant both my brother-in-law and I were each 100% responsible for the tax debt, and it was in the tens of thousands of dollars. With an income of $350/week, all I could do was sit back and watch G-d do something on my behalf that I had no way of doing for myself.

Lessons Learned

- Always let the customer confirm why they purchase your product before you leave a sale. In doing so, they solidify the reason for their decision after leaving the interaction.

- Always ask for the sale/goal if you are going to make the sale/goal happen.

- If we believe our lives are not some random accident and we are put here by our creator with a plan and purpose, then we can believe that everything happens with purpose.

- I didn't love selling vacuums, but if I saw the job

as having a purpose for a greater end, then I could sell with all my might. Selling vacuums door-to-door taught me how to be a salesman. Selling Prudential insurance taught me how to sell on a more professional level. Selling water purification systems taught me how to sell high-ticket items. Doing what I didn't love prepared me for what I do love—to own and operate my own business.

- With all the events in my life used to prepare me, I still failed. What we learn in failure is more than what we learn in success.

- A man made a million-dollar mistake in the company he worked for and was called into the boss's office. When he walked in he said "no need to say anything, I know, I'm fired." The boss asked him why he thought he should fire him after he just invested a million dollars in training him.

- Pride is when you forget where you came from; when you're under the illusion that you are an Island and that all you have accomplished is by your own hand. Pride is essentially the belief that you are above G-d.

- *For me, money was an end to be achieved. In its proper place, money is a means to an end that is worthy to be achieved.* That end is something beyond yourself.

Chapter Four
Defining Moment #2

I would attend meetings with loan brokers and bankers... listen as they talked about NOI's, ROI's, debt coverage ratios, LTV's, cost of goods, gross profits, income-to-debt ratios, P&L's and negative amortization. I had no idea what any of it meant, but I was street smart, so I bluffed my way through.

The year was now 1989. I was working for a local radio station as a third-shift DJ and advertising salesman. I had just read a book by Kenneth Hagin titled, "Following G-d's Plan for Your Life." Not only was the content of the book significant, the mere fact that I read and completed this book was a monumental feat at this point in my life. Other than the bible, this was the first book I had ever read. After finishing the book, I knew my life was about to change.

Early one morning, while sitting at church, I told G-d I wanted what He wanted for my life. I informed Him I would sit in the children's nursery alone and pray until He gave me direction. I began by asking if I was supposed to leave my current employment at the radio station. After waiting and praying most of the morning, I finally received direction; it was time to leave. Now I needed to know where to go.

He brought to mind a man I had only known for a short time. For the purpose of his family's privacy, I will just call him David. David was involved in various ministry activities and we met while participating in an event.

He was a successful apartment developer who worked his way up from nothing to owning and managing 1,836 multi-family apartment units in 13 different communities. Not only did David own and manage all the apartments, he also built each one.

I continued to pray until I had peace in my heart to call. The phone rang, David answered. I spoke, "David, I have never done this before, but I've been praying, and I believe I'm supposed to work for you." There was a long pause that seemed to last an hour. Finally, David replied, "Brother, I don't have anything for you to do." I said it was OK and thanked him for taking my call. When I hung up, I felt like an idiot, but I knew it was something I needed to do.

I was so convinced he was going to hire me that I put in my notice at the radio station and left in good standing. To make an income until he would call, I began putting roofs on houses again.

During that time, upon hearing I had left the radio station, several businesses I had sold advertising to offered me positions with their companies. I turned them all down. I didn't want them to spend money training me, only for me to leave when David would call; and he would call, I just knew it.

It was a cold, dark morning at 6:00am, standing in my driveway waiting for my ride to take me to the job site. I was wearing jeans and a sweatshirt, a heavy coat and gloves. I looked up at the stars and cried out, "Lord, there are people who hate wearing suits and ties, they call them monkey suits. They wouldn't be caught dead working in an office. Lord I want to wear a suit and work in an office. Give me that job and give this one to someone who wants it." Months had gone by and no call had come.

Then, one rainy Wednesday night, I felt I was being robbed of what I was promised from G-d. On our way home from church, Jenny and I took a turn and went to the offices of David's company. We stood out in the pouring rain, laid hands on the building and began to pray, claiming what was promised would be ours.

David called the next day. Within a week I was officially employed.

Earlier in this chapter I mentioned David built 1,836 units in 13 different communities. All the properties were doing well, running at a 90% or better occupancy and they were all making money and all the loan payments were current.

The problem was this: in 1990 the Savings & Loans, known as the S&L's, were dropping like flies. He had construction loans that had become due, and there weren't any banks to take out the loans. Does this sound familiar? As bad as it sounds, it was relatively mild compared to the banking problems of 2008.

We are experiencing today, on a large scale, what was happening 2 decades ago on a smaller scale. In response to the crisis, the government formed the Resolution Trust Corporation (RTC). They were the ones who managed the failed S&Ls until the assets could be liquidated and the loans sold off. David hired me to find financing for these 13 communities. I sat across the desk from him as he asked me about my experience with banks. All I could think of was my last experience in a bank, making a deal not to go to jail over check kiting.

He hired me anyway. In that time of terrible crisis, he hired me, with no experience and no education. He took more than just a chance on me; this didn't even make sense. My salary was $450 a week plus a bonus of $1,500 each time I closed a loan. I had never made $1,500 at one time in my life.

My first task was to memorize the names of the 13 communities, what towns they were in, who the lenders were, and how much the loans were on each property. I sat at my new desk, completely overwhelmed. *How can I ever remember this,* I thought, *much less find millions in loan dollars?*

I was taken back to the day I was studying for my life insurance license, how the Lord changed everything and opened my mind to understand and retain the material. I prayed again.

This was the beginning of my mind truly being restored from the days of being burnt out on drugs. I began to remember enormous amounts of information. To this day, I have the uncanny ability to remember numbers effortlessly.

Father-Mentor-Best Friend

I was sitting on the floor of the file room trying to locate Deeds of Trust, General Warranty Deeds, Certificates of Occupancy and construction budgets for each property when David walked in. I said to him, "Boy David, this is hard." He said, **"Easy doesn't pay much."** Simple as the saying was, this was the first time a man walked into my life, just like he walked in that file room, and spoke words of advice to me. This was one of the many, many things I would learn from this man.

In my first week at the company, David called me in his office. "Dean, do you remember the day you showed me how nice your car looked after you had just detailed it? You need to do the same thing for yourself, you need to detail yourself."

Then he said something even more profound at this point in my life. "Dean, you are successful. You work for a successful company; that makes you successful. I wouldn't have hired you if I didn't believe that." I had waited my whole life to hear those words. It took me right back to the days when I would ask my mother if anyone in our family was ever successful. I was 28 years old, and a very successful man was telling me I was a success.

He told me I needed to look successful. He taught me the basic things a father would teach his son. He explained how I should wear undershirts beneath white shirts and only wear long sleeve shirts. He taught me to wear socks tall enough to cover my legs in case I was to cross them in a business meeting. He taught me to always take off my suit jacket when in a car so as to not wrinkle the back. He taught me the value of a professional haircut. As if this wasn't enough, he preceded to hand me his credit card. "Go to a men's shop and purchase two suits with two pairs of pants. This way you have four suits by mixing them up. Have the salesman pick out ties and shirts for each suit. Then, buy three pairs of shoes, a pair of slip-ons, wing tip shoes and a pair of wing-tip slip-ons with tassels."

Let me stop and remind you that I grew up without a father or even a father-figure in my life. I always longed for someone to take me in and show me how life works; someone to teach me the ways of business and believe in me. At the age of 28, I was a father myself to three boys and I finally had someone who treated me like a son.

I would sit in his office for hours a day, soaking in what he had to teach. He recounted his start-up stories and taught me how to use and eventually depend on my Day-Timer. (The Day-Timer was eventually replaced by the Black Berry, which has now been replaced by my IPhone). He taught me to always keep a legal pad in my desk drawer and write down whom I spoke with on the phone, what we spoke about and when. In this way, I always had a record to look back on.

He didn't believe in an 80-hour workweek; I couldn't have agreed with him more. Of all the books I've read in my life, when someone proposes the need for 12-16 hour days 7 days a week, I begin to doubt their authority on the matter. At least for those with families, working these kinds of hours means sacrificing something greater (your family) for something lesser (business success).

He explained that, while he did not work more than 50 hours a week, he believed every hour he worked should count. He believed in working **harder and smarter**. "As long as you are working, however many hours you are working, make it count for the most it can," he would say.

David's wisdom often came in the simplest forms. **One day he drew a diagram of 4 smiley faces in a row and one sad face.** "The smiley faces are people like your landlord, the bank and the utility company. They all get paid so they are smiling. The sad face is you, because by the time you pay everyone else, there's nothing left for you." He said it wouldn't be long before I was making good money and right away I needed to begin putting some away from each bonus I would get. By doing this I would be paying myself first.

He then drew a picture of a pond. "You should eventually work to create a pond of income and work on growing that pond. Then, each week take a certain amount from the pond to live on. If you have a great month, continue to only take the specified amount out of the pond so it will grow. If you ever have bad months, you won't feel it because you will still be taking the same amount out of the pond." I am always teaching this principle, especially to those who are self employed. Without this principle at work in your life, you stay on a financial rollercoaster, and the impact is compounded if you work for yourself. I will speak of the pond more extensively in Part II of this book.

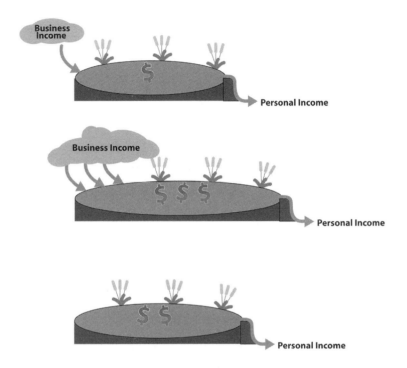

One day he illustrated a baseball diamond. He explained this represented a little league field. "The game is played by a pitcher who throws the ball to a batter, who then tries to run all three bases and finally to home."

He then drew a bigger diamond. "This is a major league field and the game is played by a pitcher who throws the ball to a batter, who then tries to run all three bases and then to home."

"Do you know the difference between little league and major league? The game is essentially the same; the difference is in the size of the field they play on. Dean, you are in the big leagues now.

I've often considered how people think of themselves dictates what they do and, in terms of their economy, how much they earn. If you work in a country club in the Catskills, you bring your customer their drinks, take their orders, bring their food and clear their table. Your tips range between $20 and $100. If you work for a diner, you do the same exact work for tips that range between one and five dollars. Why do some choose to work at a diner and some at a country club? It is not because of the work, but because of how they see themselves. See greater value in yourself and the work you do will have greater value as well.

Years ago, an experiment was performed where an ad was placed in the paper offering a job paying $15,000 annually. This was a time when a person could survive on a salary of that amount. The ad did not describe the job, only the pay. Quite a few answered the ad.

Another ad was placed in the same paper; it offered an annual salary of $25,000. Many people answered the ad, but the number was fewer than before.

This continued until the salary offered was $50,000, a very large amount at the time. Very few people inquired for that position.

Since the ad gave no job description, the response rate directly correlated to people's sense of self worth and what they assumed their value was to a company.

T. Harv Eker further illustrates this point in his book, "Secrets of the Millionaire Mind."

He explains that we have a financial thermostat which regulates what we earn based on our belief system. A thermostat in a room set at 70 degrees will keep that room at 70 degrees even if it gets hotter or colder during the course of the day. Likewise, our internal, financial thermostats keep us making the same amount each year, even if we have windfalls one month or financial losses the next, according to the book. The thermostat gets its setting based on the grid through which you see wealth. Change your perception of self worth and you can raise your financial thermostat.

I was beginning to see myself in a way I never had. I was seeing myself through the eyes of someone who believed in me. My thermostat was beginning to go higher. And herein lies another important point for our personal economy. The wealth we build when we build up others is far reaching and has exponential results. By giving me a chance, and seeing in me something I couldn't see myself, David gave me something far more valuable than a job, he gave me a vision for my life I never had before.

One of the most valuable things David ever taught me was **Live to Give.** His passion for making money was second to his passion for giving it away. He loved to bless people and he did it without any fan fair. Nobody knew the kinds of money he was giving away.

He gave away free apartments in every community to people who could not afford one or to someone whose house burned down. He refused to lease our company cars; instead he purchased all our cars and gave them to those in need when we were done with them. He had a special checking account where he put tens of thousands of dollars to give away each month. He showed me the meaning of why we should desire to be successful, to be a blessing to others.

I began very quickly to love this man as a father. I didn't work for the money; at least that wasn't my motivation. I wanted to bless this man who had done so much for me and, if I was successful in securing these loans, I could play a part in saving his company.

This all seemed so crazy; I was so far out of my league. I thought, *if people knew who I really was, it would have been comical.* He told me that I was in the Major Leagues, heck, I was the kid who was always picked last for baseball.

I would attend meetings with loan brokers and bankers, day timer in hand. I would listen as they talked about NOI's, ROI's, debt coverage ratios, LTV's, cost of goods, gross profits, income-to-debt ratios, P&L's, negative amortization and on and on. I had no idea what any of it meant, but I was street wise, so I bluffed my way through the meeting. When we finished, I would run back to my office, look up all the terms and learn what they meant and how I was to use them in securing loans.

I remember finding myself on the top floor of an attorney's office in Up-Town Charlotte. All the bank vice presidents were present as we were fighting for our life not to be foreclosed on. The loans were due and we could not find lenders to take them out. All of a sudden, a man turned to me as said, "What do you think Dean?" I sat there, frozen in time. *What do I think? If you had any idea who I am, you wouldn't care what I think. I'm an ex druggie from Andover NY. I graduated 36 in a class of 36; what do I think?* I came back to real time and answered the question and they were satisfied. That day, I realized G-d put me in the position I was in and gave me favor. **I have learned to covet the favor of G-d as my most valuable asset.** Today, it is the favor of G-d that has allowed me to secure loans for others in a time when banks are not lending money. During an unprecedented time in banking history, I have secured spec loans, loans on model homes built to sell other homes, and land loans. This is impossible in the natural. It is only possible by "Doing Business Supernaturally," something we will talk about later.

After two years with David, the favor of G-d had allowed me to find financing on all 13 properties. We didn't lose one of them, and now we were ready to start building again.

Lessons Learned

- Pay yourself first
- Decide which size field you want to play in
- Live out of your reserves
- Easy doesn't pay much
- Work harder and smarter
- The Favor of G-d is your most valuable asset
- Pay attention to your financial thermostat

Chapter Five

Movin' on Up

There is something far greater than money, and that
is a friend who will take you in, love you for who you are and
give of himself to see you become something better.
If you find this, you are wealthy.

Learning to have vision

David and I were sitting in his father's truck one evening after a rezoning meeting when he turned and asked a question that took me by surprise.

"Where do you see yourself in five years, Dean?"

For many people, this is a normal question. You only need take one step beyond the what-I-want-to-be-when-I'm-big question. Not only had I never been asked this question, I had never considered my future in these terms period.

Yes, I always had dreams. I wanted to be a rock star, which by now the door seemed to be closing, even though I did eventually learn to play guitar. I always wanted to be successful, but I never had a plan on how to get there. And now I am being asked where I see myself in five years.

I stammered for a minute, and finally, somewhat embarrassed, admitted I didn't understand the question or know what kind of an answer he was looking for. He clarified and asked me how much money I wanted to be making in five years, and where I saw myself in the company? I thought of the most money I could try to imagine myself making and said, "I would like to be working for the company in five years and making $50,000 a year." Then came the fear—*I hope he doesn't think that is too much.*

That night I contemplated the question and my response. I didn't even have the vision to think of being promoted; all I said was, "I would like to be working for the company in five years." Suddenly something came over me. I started regretting saying $50,000 and, believe it or not, I called him. "David, I would like to be making $100,000 in five years." Remember, in the introduction I said I got where I am today, not because of me, but in spite of me. I think you're catching on by now.

After securing financing for the 13 properties there was not much work for me to do. A couple of properties were not doing as well as the others, so in addition to finding the construction financing for new properties we were building, I became a property manager, overseeing the struggling communities.

Once again, I had G-d's favor. Like with the financing, I had no property management experience and yet, I kept coming up with good ideas to improve occupancy. As time went on, I was given more and more properties to oversee. Eventually, a decision was made to promote me to oversee all the properties. Each community had a manager on site. That manager answered to a property manager, each of whom had three or four properties to oversee. These property managers all reported to me.

I remember asking David if I could have a car phone, as I was traveling so much. He bought me a $900 car phone. It was so expensive because you could disconnect the receiver from the car, go to the trunk and take out the dictionary-sized battery, put it in a sack that you could carry, plug the phone into it and walk around outside your car with your phone. Wow, what a great idea, I wonder if it will catch on?

Make it or Break it on the size of your butter patty

One day David said he had something to show me. He told me his original 5-year plan was to build 1,500 apartments and make a specific amount of income each month. He explained how he actually built 336 more units than planned, but he was making a little more than half of what he planned.

When he told me this, I made it my personal project to figure out a solution to his dilemma. Once again, I had favor. Ideas were flooding my mind. I saw each community operating autonomously, keeping us from taking advantage of our large buying power.

There is an expression, "A restaurant will either make it or break it, based on the size of its butter patty." If the patty is too big, then you are not paying attention to the little things, you're letting the expenses run away on you. If the patty is too small, then you are ripping your customers off and not giving them enough for their money. Ultimately, they won't come back. You are either going to lose on the income side or the expense side if you are not looking out for the little things. If you look after the little things, the big things will take care of themselves. In the Bible, Proverbs 27: 23-24 explains that you must be diligent to know the state of your flocks and pay attention to your herds, because riches are not forever; therefore, don't take what you have for granted and become slack.

It is much easier to get sloppy when things are going good since you don't need to look after every penny. Then, all of a sudden, one day you find you have been dealing with a slack hand and have lost much, possibly everything.

Don't wait until things are tight to evaluate the size of your butter patty. If you look closely at what you spend and where you spend it when times are good, you will be much more profitable in good times, and better equipped to endure lean times.

This fact is true in both your personal finances as well as your business finances.

Reduce and consolidate expenses

I decided to take on the expenses first. We met monthly with all the managers. We would give out awards and bonus checks, talk about our challenges and what our victories were for the month.

Each property bought all their printing supplies from a local printer: leases, applications, maintenance notices etc. I engaged a local, first-year printer and we developed a system. We established how many items we would always need on hand with ceilings and floors so we never had too much or too little. He visited once a month and replenished what we needed.

Rather than each manager ordering their own forms at top dollar, sometimes with overnight shipping costs, they simply picked up what they needed each month after our meeting from the home office.

I contacted a paint company and negotiated a price per gallon that was less than half of what we were paying individually at each property by giving them the entire portfolios business. I even negotiated free shipping based on the volume of business we were doing.

Since many of the properties were rather new, the maintenance men were performing mostly menial tasks like picking up trash and cleaning apartments. This was not the case on all the properties but certainly on the newest ones. As a result, I bought each property a paint sprayer and carpet cleaning machines. We subbed out the trash pickup and apartment cleaning, which we could hire out cheap, and had our maintenance men turn the vacant apartments, significantly reducing our turn cost.

I brought in several insurance companies to bid on our business, which ended up reducing our insurance overhead by nearly half.

Optimized Income

Next, I went to work on the income side of things. I noticed our bonus system rewarded the managers, leasing agents and maintenance men, but not for the things that were critical to the profitability of the company.

I increased the overall bonus, which made everyone happy, but broke it down into three parts, each part being a goal that we as a company wanted accomplished. This new bonus system put everyone in the company on the same page in terms of what we were shooting for each month.

When all these changes were implemented, we reached our NOI goal. By then I knew that NOI stood for Net Operating Income (the amount you make after expenses, before debt service).

At this point, I was then promoted to Vice-President of the company. I had a company car and was making over $100,000 a year—nobody had ever treated me so good, given me so much opportunity, taught me so much and believed in me like David did.

Say Goodbye to the Debt

With the new promotion and the increased income, I was finally at a place to pay off my old debts, just as I believed I had heard the Lord say I would. I called all my creditors and, one by one, paid off the balances. I then negotiated with the IRS and agreed on an offer and compromise and paid them $32,000. After they were paid, I paid off the State of NY. My last stop was a call I had been waiting for years to make—I called my old church. I told them what G-d had done in my life and I sent them a check and paid them back the deposit on the carpet. I was living out in that moment what was only a faith dream years earlier.

All this had come to pass because I listened to the voice of the Lord that day in the church nursery, that voice in my spirit that impressed me to call David for a job.

Bubble Belly is Born

While working for this company was a major blessing in my life, far more than I ever dreamed, I was still the vice president of someone else's company. I did not have the liberty of hiring my children to teach them business. As a result, I worked with them to start their own company. I knew the great value it was to start my own business at such a young age and I wanted them to have the same experience. The only difference was, they would have a father to watch over them and guide them.

At the time, we had four children: Daniel was 16, with his driver's license, David was 14, Andrew was 11 and Lizzie was 5.

My idea was to start a vending business. I purchased five large gumball machines with a capacity for hundreds of gumballs. When dispensed they would travel down a spiral and be retrieved at the bottom.

The children did virtually everything else themselves. They came up with their own name (Bubble Belly Gumballs) and worked with a graphic artist to design the logo, a big gumball machine with eyes and a mouth on the oversized bubble head and arms. They had business cards made and opened a checking account. They went to stores and restaurants, pitching storeowners on the idea of putting a machine in their location. They negotiated terms. They would pay a flat monthly fee or a percentage of sales, or use the cute-kid-learning-business card and get the owner to allow them in for free.

I helped them design some very simple spreadsheets to keep track of the income and gumball usage from each location. They tracked their numbers, utilized the spreadsheets and ran the reports. Each week they would go out to service their investments. Daniel drove to the locations. David put the gumballs in the top of the machine while Andrew took the money out of the bottom of the machine. Lizzie would take her little bottle cleaner and cloth and clean the machines.

The kids decided on a monthly salary for themselves. The rest of the income would go back into the company to buy more machines. Once they saved enough to purchase another machine, they gave themselves a raise. Partly because another unit meant more money, and partly because another unit meant more work.

During the same time Bubble Belly was getting off the ground I was visiting a 250-unit apartment community we had recently built. I spent the day working with management. Another community built at the same time, just down the road from us, was hurting our occupancy. By the end of the day, we had contrived several ideas to get an edge on the competition.

Later that evening I was having our regularly scheduled Bubble Belly meeting with the children. Reviewing the monthly income reports, it was obvious one of our best selling units was operating at half its normal capacity. They told me the lobby of the Chinese restaurant where the machine was put in other machines.

We brainstormed and came up with the idea of putting several "winner" gumballs where they could easily be seen in the machine. We would put a sign on the unit saying "get a winner gumball and get lunch on us." That idea put our sales back on track the very next month.

It was a great opportunity to show the children it doesn't matter if you are dealing with a multi-million dollar apartment community or a twenty-five cent gumball, the principles in business are the same.

Eventually, the children grew the 5 machines into 12 machines, selling candy in addition to gumballs. By the end, they sold the business for a profit. Years later, when Andrew went off to college, he bought the business back from the person we sold it to, and he ran it with a friend for extra income. They added even more machines and sold it again after he graduated college. He used the money to go to Argentina and get married to the girl he had been dating for over 3 years. On and off, that business was in our family for over 10 years.

ABCD America's Best Chinese Delivers

Deep inside, there was always a longing in me to own a restaurant. That's why I was so excited when we started looking for a business we could grow, coast to coast, without the large debt inherent with the apartment industry and decided on developing a chain of Chinese delivery restaurants. We wanted to do for Chinese food what Domino's had done for pizza. Tom Monagham made delivery synonymous with pizza. We were determined to do the same for Chinese food.

I came up with ABCD, **Americas Best Chinese Delivers.** I even came up with a full alphabet acronym.

Americas

Best

Chinese

Delivers

Excellent

Fantastic

Great

Hot

Incredible

Juicy

…you get the drift.

I had the time of my life planning the restaurant with David. Down to every detail, my heart was in it. I was excited about overseeing the qualified people we had who looked after everything, from the computer cashier system that sent the orders to the kitchen, to developing the recipes. From designing the layout of the restaurant to learning how to cook the food ourselves at The Culinary Institute of America in Hyde Park, NY; this was the vein I somehow always knew was waiting for me.

I remember walking through the first restaurant the day before we opened, running my fingers over the stainless steel tables and thinking, "this is what I was born for. We are going coast to coast and I am going to be another Ray Kroc or Dave Thomas."

I felt destiny had found me. This was it, this was my destiny, this was going to happen and I was going to make my mark on the world. I even had my license plate changed to ABCD.

As it turned out, our first location was up and running with the second underway when David pulled the plug. He told me he was an apartment developer, not a restaurateur and he needed his vice president working on expanding the portfolio, not spending 80 hours a week in a single restaurant.

I put down the phone and took our last order. I walked back to the kitchen, made the order myself, brought it out front and took the customer's money. I followed the customer to the door and locked it behind them.

All I could feel was failure. It took me a long time to recover. My purpose in life had been taken away and I was disillusioned as to what my purpose really was. It had really taken the wind out of my sail. There was an empty place in me after that for a very long time.

Scene Two: Enter Pride... Again

By 1993, I had built my own home. It was a beautiful five-bedroom, two and a half bath, brick home with an in-ground swimming pool and was gorgeously landscaped. While this was a blessing on one level, pride was beginning to enter my heart, again.

In 1995 my wife had given birth to our last son Christopher; we were now a family of 7. With salary and bonuses I had years making upwards of $185K. I was riding a wave of success that lasted a decade and I thought there was no way I could crash.

Unfortunately, like in times past, my focus had left the Lord and was back on myself.

I learned many invaluable life lessons during this time; I believed that the Lord was my provider and that the company I worked for was the source of his provision. I learned, through example, the reason for success was to give to others. On one hand, I had been humbled by the love and generosity of this father figure in my life, and learned many principles through my time with David. With all this knowledge, however, there was still a problem in my heart. I became consumed, once again, with the house I lived in and the car I drove. I was consumed by how many apartment communities we owned and the part I played in leading the team that took the company from 1836 units to 6,000 units by the time I left.

Once again, my focus had gotten back to what I had and not who I was, or better said, whose I was.

On February 1st 1999, after almost 10 years together, David and I split. In my heart I knew it was time for us to go our separate ways; still, it was a difficult time in my life. Our split meant I was losing a good friend. He gave me a very generous severance pay and we parted.

We met a couple times soon after for coffee and I told him about my plans of opening a coast to coast chain of Bagel Deli's. Four months later, around the first of June I met with him for the last time. I told him I was getting ready to open my first restaurant in just two weeks, on June 14th and he should come by. He had just finished the new offices that we had worked together on for years. He gave me a tour and we hugged and said good-bye.

On June 14th I opened the deli on schedule and then received a phone call that his plane had gone down with his wife, our construction manager and the pilot on board. I shut the deli and sped to the airport, thinking the whole way that this cannot really be happening. When I arrived, it was confirmed that there were no survivors. The agony I felt that day was like no other in my life.

There are still many times, almost 15 years later that I think about him when I am in a tough business situation. I often ask myself, *what would David have done?* As I have become successful in my businesses, I have wanted, on many occasions, to be able to sit and talk with him and tell him what has happened in my life, the way we used to do so many times.

It is my privilege to share some of the lessons he taught me, so that others can learn from him as well.

Lessons Learned

- Businesses make it or break it based on the size of their butter patty. If the patty is too big, you are not looking after your cost and there is waste in other parts of the business. If the patty is too small, you are not looking after the customers' needs and they will eventually leave you for someone who is.

- The time to look at the butter patty is when your business is doing well, not when it is struggling.

When times are good, it is easy to overlook waste. Pay attention before it is too late.

- If you work for someone else, come up with creative ideas to help your children learn to be entrepreneurs.

- Live a life of faith, believing that what is impossible with man is possible with G-d.

- There is something far greater than money, and that is a friend who will take you in, love you for who you are and give of himself to see you become something better. If you find this, you are wealthy.

- Remember where you came from and don't let pride enter in. Pride comes before a fall. If you were born with a silver spoon in your mouth, and remembering where you came from doesn't help, then realize it is your parents that were successful when you were a child, not you.

I love the scene on the TV show "The Cosby's." Vanessa was complaining to her dad that the other kids in school were making fun of her because she was rich. He told her not to be deceived, her parents were rich; she wasn't.

Bragging because your parents are rich is like bragging because you are tall, as though you had anything to do with it.

Chapter Six
Self Employment Revisited - Crash #2

This was my first attempt at building something from scratch by myself. No boss and no partner, just me—sink or swim. I had VIP's from the community come, the newspaper, politicians, close friends and people from my church.

The Need to Feed

I guess it all started when I was only about 8 years old. I was visiting my Aunt Lou and Uncle Frank in Mahopac, NY. They owned a small restaurant and I fell in love immediately.

Sitting at the bar, a man walked up to pay and asked for a cigar. As Uncle Frank reached into the cigar box, I heard a loud, jovial voice, "come on Frank, and give me one from the bottom of the box." When he left, I asked my uncle why he said that. "When you open a new box, you put the old ones from the previous box on top to sell first, so the fresh ones are on the bottom." He then explained how he reversed the process, since most people know this technique. This way he still sold the older ones first.

This moment stuck in my thoughts my entire life and the desire to own my own restaurant never left me. Later in life, I found out my father had also owned a restaurant as one of his many businesses.

The day I left David's company, I drove home, and, after telling my wife and children what had happened, I went to work on **Stein Bagel & Deli.** I was going to fulfill my dream of owning a coast-to-coast chain of restaurants.

Creative juices started to flow

I was on a roll. Once again, I knew I could not go this alone. I needed divine guidance. Some would say that they sought a higher power. **I don't understand why you would go to a higher power when you can go straight to the highest power.**

I prayed, "Lord, where do I even begin?" I grabbed a legal pad and began writing down the flood of thoughts that ensued.

There were hundreds of aspects to be considered: a name, what the deli would offer, the set up and layout of the store, a policy and procedure manual and on and on.

Having been through the process of ABCD, I had experience, but this time I was on my own. I didn't have a team of talented experienced people to oversee. I was chief cook and bottle washer of this operation.

When the dream is conceived, you imagine the finished product not far off. Then you start and realize a simple, unnoticed aspect of your business requires literally dozens of decisions be made. Think about the following for a moment. You decide to sell coffee in your deli. A simple decision, not much to think about, right? Wrong!

1. What brand of coffee should I purchase?

2. Pre-ground or whole bean?

3. How many different flavors of coffee should I carry?

4. What method should I use to brew the coffee?

5. What method should I use to dispense the coffee?

6. What size cups should I offer?

7. How many sizes should I offer?

8. What kind of cups should I use?

9. What kind of lids do I choose?

10. Do I need heat sleeves for the cups?

11. What do I charge per cup?

12. What do I use for cream, liquid, powder, both?

13. What do I use for sugar, Sweet n Low, Equal, in packets, in a container?

14. What stir sticks do I choose, plastic, wood?

We are talking about a mere cup of coffee. Can you imagine

all the choices, all the decisions that have to be made, have to be thought out and figured out? I loved every minute of it.

I am getting ahead of myself, let me back up. The first step was to decide where to locate the deli.

I picked a new retail strip center right behind a major hospital. We were sandwiched between the large regional hospital and all the doctor offices in a medical park. The site was close to a major interstate and had a classy look to it.

Looking back, and hindsight is always 20/20, I should have considered the fact that the center did not have an anchor tenant.

With the location secured, I hired an architect for the interior design. We worked together closely, covering every detail. I envisioned the exact look and flow, the flow of the kitchen to the flow of the employees at the front counter, to the flow of the customers. Then I hired a company to do the build out.

Every detail was important: the color scheme, the kind of tables and chairs and the type booths. We had to decide what our menu boards would look like, what kind of flooring, ceiling and lighting, whether customers would be given their drinks or get their own.

There were technical items as well: the cash register system, being Visa and Master Card capable. We needed towel vendors, food vendors, drink vendors, welcome mats and anti fatigue mats.

What equipment could we get away with buying used, and what we should purchase new? We needed to decide the size of our freezer and walk in cooler, and how much stainless steel prep table space we would need.

And the mother of it all, what method of bagel making should we use—boil or steam?

Wow, can you feel your blood rushing as your heart gets pumping, just thinking about all the details?

We needed a logo, so I hired a good friend who I had helped get into business for himself. He had run the newspaper that the previous company I worked for owned and when the decision was made to shut the paper down, I made the suggestion to sell all the equipment to him in a way that he could afford so he could start his own business. He was quite talented and is still operating that same business he started over 15 years ago.

He designed a logo that made our name STEIN, look like the rays over a sun coming up, Stein Bagel and Deli.

He then designed the wallpaper you saw when you first walked in. The wallpaper had bagels on it. What no one knew

North Branch Center
970 Branchview Dr., NE
Concord, NC 28025
704. 786.4755
Fax 704.784.4688

was that he could not find the graphics for the bagels so he blew up lifesavers and put sesame seeds on them. This wallpaper would be used in all our stores, coast to coast.

Now that we had a logo, we could have uniforms designed. We also came up with a great lighted sign for the front of the store and had menus printed.

We hired Neva Burns whose husband Dane I had gone to high school with back in NY. They were now living in the same town as I was in NC. She was an excellent cook. She developed all our recipes for our five different salads and seven different cream cheeses, and designed our 15 different sandwiches. The menu was exquisite. She went with us to the food shows and along with my wife, we picked out the soups we wanted and the cheesecakes and all different meats and cheeses, etc.

Ready, Set, Go

Then came the day of reckoning, Saturday, June 12th. I invited about 50 people to the deli the Saturday night before the scheduled grand opening that following Monday the 14th. I wanted to see if the procedures we set up and practiced would actually work. Would the work on one side of the counter flow and make a good experience for the customers on the other side of the counter?

Would our setup allow customers to comfortably and naturally order, pay, get their drinks and find a table?

I was nervous. This was my first attempt at building something from scratch, by myself. No boss and no partner, just me— sink or swim. I sat back and watched as it all came together. I had

VIP's from the community come, close friends, the newspaper, politicians and people from my church. It went incredibly well and my grand opening jitters were put to rest. I was ready.

A Family Affair

Daniel, my oldest son, had just graduated high school. I wanted to teach him the business. When we first opened the deli, he only made the bagels. He didn't realize it then, but he had an entre-preneurial spirit of his own. He began making other items on his own, such as bagel chips and new menu items. He eventually took over the entire kitchen and allowed us to eliminate a posi-tion, saving us labor overhead.

David and Andrew, my two other sons, worked at the food station and register while Lizzie, our 8-year-old daughter, even had her own uniform and went around cleaning tables. My mother-in-law, Karen, came to work for us as well. It truly was a family affair. We would have had our youngest son, Chris, working for us as well, however, he was only four years old, and we were concerned about child labor laws. Lizzie, at eight, was pushing it.

Right from the start, the plan was to be a coast-to-coast chain. Everything we did was carefully thought out so as to be uniform and replicated in our stores throughout the nation. Everything was labeled, from the food items in the cooler and freezer to the paper products in the counters. Everything had its own proce-dure, with an opening and closing checklist. We had systems for ordering food to ensure enough without incurring waste. We even had a procedure and design for sandwich creation. Most restaurants place the tomato and lettuce together on their sandwiches. Frustratingly, you usually end up with a sandwich that slides apart. Our sandwiches were so big that we kept the lettuce and tomato on opposite sides of the meat and finished it off with two elegant toothpicks, with olives in them to keep the whole thing together. This became our signature look, which ended up on our posters and billboards.

Reinventing retail scheduling

Having worked for McDonalds and a super market as a teenager, I was well aware of the scheduling problems plaguing businesses that hire teenagers and part-time employees. It seemed people were always changing their schedules or, on occasion, just not showing up. I realized the problem was caused more by the employer than the employee. When you post a schedule less than a week in advance, you assume the employee has no life and will always adjust to your needs. I created two alternate schedules that always stayed the same. Week one gave half the employees the weekend off. In week two, the other employees had the weekend off. My crew never asked for the weekend off, they could always look at the schedule and plan around it. This schedule was fixed and everyone, including me, knew what to expect.

My design was ingenious—I would change part time scheduling, industry wide. Unfortunately no one wants to imitate you when you have a single location and it fails, even if the idea is a great one.

When I was in NY in the furniture business, I failed because I didn't know what I was doing and had no budget, no plan, no set of books and so on. This time it was different. I failed with everything in place.

I really had it all down. On a day-to-day basis I could tell you what my labor cost was, my food cost, how many of each sandwich I sold and how much food I had to throw away. Our sanitation score was always 98% or better. We were lean and mean and still failing.

At the onset of Stein Bagel & Deli, I put aside a year's income for myself. I could work at the deli and not have to take anything from it.

I decided to work in the first store as the manager for one full year for several reasons. First, I wanted to make sure the deli made it and was profitable. Secondly, I wanted to find out what mistakes I made. My plan was to build out many more stores and

I wanted to duplicate success, not failure. Thirdly, I wanted to know firsthand what it took to operate the deli. This way I would know what I could expect from my managers; I would know whether I was asking too much of them or not enough.

After having this experience under my belt, my goal was to write a Policy and Procedure Manual that was so detailed that I could hand it to someone and they could go out and start a Stein Bagel & Deli. They would know what equipment to purchase, how to set up the store and how much it would cost to build it out. They would know what and how much of each item to order. They would have the marketing and the training of the employees worked out for them. A person could work in a Stein Bagel & Deli in NC and go to one in NY and hit the ground running, knowing exactly where everything was located.

I borrowed as little money as possible, putting much of my own cash into the cost of the up-fit and equipment. I even put away six months operating capital just to make sure the business was not undercapitalized.

Crash # 2

With all the precautions, all the safeguards and all the planning, I lacked one thing; a sufficient amount of customers.

In business, you make money in two ways, in buying and selling. These two ways affect your bottom line, on the income side and on the expense side. Remember the butter patty in chapter five? I had the expense side of things down but I couldn't seem to get the income side to work. I advertised, had billboards, and even went door to door with samples and gifts to all the surrounding businesses.

My location had both a positive side and a negative side. It was in a new strip mall. It had a right hand turn in and out, heading toward a major interstate. On the other hand, there were several other sandwich type restaurants in the vicinity.

I think the biggest mistake was the lack of an anchor tenant, something like an upscale supermarket. Our breakfast crowd was good and our lunch crowd was positive, but our in between time was dead. No one came in on impulse because people weren't in that area for other reasons besides to eat. We were a destination point and bagels were just not on the radar for enough people in Concord, North Carolina.

As I write this book, over 10 years later, there are still no bagel deli restaurants in that town.

Nobly Accept Defeat... But Never Give In

The deli, which opened June 14th 1999, closed its doors on February 1st, 2001. I tried everything I could think to make this dream of mine work. Having learned from the HIS Company days, I knew the answer was not to open more stores. On the other hand, there was another lesson that I was about to learn, KNOW WHEN TO QUIT.

As I mentioned before, I had set aside a year's worth of income for myself, and six months' operating capital. If I had stopped when the money ran out, I would have walked away down, but not out.

Instead, I made one of the biggest mistakes of my life. With excellent credit and relationships with bankers, I kept borrowing money to keep the deli going. In the year that followed, after the operating capital ran out, and the six months that followed after my savings ran out, I lived on loans and credit cards.

About the time it began to be evident that the deli was not going to provide an income for me anytime soon, I was approached by an out of state businessman.

He wanted to set aside a certain amount of money to build some apartments. He was willing to lose this particular sum of money, if needed, but no more. He had calculated his losses ahead of time and then, after assessing the risk, moved forward.

During that time I found a great piece of land to build an apartment community on. A new exit was going in and a new road would make a great location for the apartments. I worked hard on the deal. I put in extensive market research, worked with architects to design the building and floor plans. I worked diligently with lenders to secure financing and everything in between. The partner's job was to supply the capital to move forward and to find investors to finance the needed equity to finish.

We were getting so close when the money ran out. My partner said it was over, that he had spent all he agreed to spend and that we would abandon the venture. We were so close; all we needed was for him to find an investor. As soon as the road was in we could begin building. I did everything I was supposed to do and now we were dead in the water. I completely disagreed with his decision, but it was his money, so there was not much I could say or do.

As it turned out, the entire road project was delayed for several years. Had he not made that wise decision to only spend what he was willing to lose, he would have lost a great deal more.

I, on the other hand, had not only lost all I had, I lost a lot more than I had. The dream of the coast-to-coast restaurant chain died just like it did with ABCD. This time, however, the reason for my crash was not due to pride, although I was about to be humbled more than I could ever have imagined.

I closed the deli by calling the very company I purchased my equipment from and sold it all back for pennies on the dollar. I watched a team disassemble my walk in cooler, my walk in freezer and my beloved bagel oven. Piece by piece, they tore apart my dream. It took a few more years, however, until I understood why I loved to feed people. This dream was much more of a calling in my life then I initially realized, and it was going to take another defining moment for this dream to come to pass.

Lesson Learned

- When the provision runs out, do not keep your endeavor alive by artificial means. In other words, set a designated time, amount of money, or some benchmark for your business to succeed. If it hasn't made it by that time, do not keep it alive by going further and further in debt or pouring more and more money into it until you're broke.

- The carrot in front of you on that stick may always be just a step away. If your expectations of making a go at it are not realized in the allotted time you pre-determined, you may be chasing the carrot straight to the poor house.

- G-d is not short on supply, if He is not supplying, you are only taking matters into your own hands by borrowing money to artificially keep something alive. Learn when it is time to fish and when it is time to cut bait.

Chapter Seven

Defining Moment #3

After rounding up a couple dollars from seat cushions, we headed out the door to see what we could get for dinner. Approaching our smashed Camry with a single hubcap and a couple bucks in change, we looked at each other and said, "How did we get here?" all we could do was laugh.

As I mentioned earlier, after we went through all of our savings, we began borrowing money. In an effort to pay off as much debt as possible, we sold our house, making an $80,000 profit, (you remember, the beautiful brick home with the big in-ground swimming pool). We sold both our new Jaguar and Suburban and even our Y2K stuff that, as it turned out, we didn't need (who knew?).

I was initially upset when we decided to move. I believed the Lord wanted me to sell but I didn't want to leave. It is one thing to know the Lord's will; it is another to trust that His will is better than yours. I told the Lord, "If you want us to move, then sell our house in 90 days. If not, I will take it off the market."

On the 90th day our house sold. If that wasn't enough, it turns out the buyer was a Messianic Jew. G-d was driving the point home; He was in the move.

One afternoon, before finding another house to live in, I was swimming in our pool alone and wondering where we might end up. In the back of my mind, I remember being plagued by the thought of what type of house we would have and what my high school friends would think.

Just then, the Lord spoke to my heart and said,

"Do you know why you care what people think about what kind of house you live in and what kind of car you drive, people you have not seen in over 20 years and whom you will likely never see again?" Before I could give an answer, He said, "It's because you see your worth in what you possess, not in who possesses you."

He went on to reveal to me that my value is not in my accomplishments, but in the very nature of who I am. I was fearfully created in my mother's womb, I am hand made by G-d Himself. I am seated in heavenly places. I was bought with a price. I am a royal priesthood, a holy nation and a chosen generation. I have value, not because of who I am, but because of whose I am. And this is not something I can change with a house, car or any earthly thing.

I cannot tell you how freeing a revelation that was. It was as if an elephant had been taken off my chest. I don't have to meet anyone's expectations, real or imaginary. I stand before G-d, no one else, and He thinks I'm pretty cool.

After that day, it didn't matter where I lived or what I drove. Today, I live in a very nice house across the street from a beautiful lake, and drive a sporty convertible. But I live where I do because my wife and I love the area, not because I care what others think. I drive the car I drive because I have always loved cool cars, not because it says who I am; my value is not defined by it. **Sometimes what is wrong in a person's life is not what he does, but why he does it**. I really have been set free from keeping up appearances.

Starting Over

After selling our home, we did eventually find a new place to live. We ended up out in the country, surrounded by forest. Ironically, I was entering a long financial "wilderness" experience, and I was to literally live out in the wilderness during this time.

I tried relentlessly to make my way as an entrepreneur. It seemed I was trying to make butter from a brick. Whatever I did ended the same as my previous attempts. I finally resolved that I would have to go back into the work force and work for someone else.

The timing of my revelation (I am worth more than the sum of what I own) could not have come at a more opportune time. We were being stripped of every possession. I came home one day and saw our great big camper beside the house and thought, "I wish they would hurry up and get this thing and be done with it." The camper was the last possession we had besides the clothes on our backs and when it was gone it was finally over.

They picked it up on Thanksgiving Day and I can honestly say we were in a process of learning how to be truly thankful.

There is a big lesson I learned during this time. *THE FEAR OF LOSING EVERYTHING IS WORSE, THAN THE REALITY OF LOSING EVERYTHING.*

An amazing freedom came after having nothing more to lose. They say it is always darkest right before the dawn. Once it gets as dark as it can get, there is nowhere to go but to a brighter place. Once we lost everything, once we hit rock bottom, there was nowhere to go but up.

We drove an old Toyota Camry, and were quite thankful when someone accidently plowed into the side of it. The insurance money paid a couple months rent.

One day, we had no food and no money. Dinner was approaching. We went through the cushions of our living room furniture; we looked all over the house for change. After rounding up a couple dollars, we headed out the door to see what we could get for dinner. Approaching our smashed Camry with a single hubcap and a couple bucks in change, we looked at each other and said, "How did we get here?" all we could do was laugh. The truth is, we had each other, our five beautiful children and my mother-in-law.

Back in the glory days, my wife's mother wanted to move to from NY to NC. We bought her a house and moved her down. When we lost everything, we also lost her house, so she moved in with us. She ended up living with us for seven years.

So, here we found ourselves, totally broke, stripped of all we had once owned and unable to be successful in any business venture we tried. I finally came to the conclusion that I was not called to be the businessman.

I decided it was time to go back to work for someone else. A part of me felt it was wrong, that I wasn't trusting G-d. But what could I do? There was no income.

I asked G-d to direct my steps, to open doors and close doors, whatever He wanted. I truly came to want His will more than my own. I didn't want to go to work for someone else, but I was willing if that is what He wanted. I would do what was prudent. I would seek employment and leave the results, either way, up to Him.

Now here's the deal: I called all the banks I had relationships with to find out if any were hiring. Then I made appointments for interviews. Pay attention here, this is what happens when you lose control and learn to trust. I only went to banks that were hiring, and banks where I had relationships with the people who did the hiring. Sounds pretty fool proof when you add the fact that I had already successfully brokered $350,000,000 in loans and I was willing to apply for entry-level to VP positions. No one would hire me.

It became very clear; I was not to go to work for someone else. *G-d always answers our prayers, sometimes with a yes and sometimes with a no. Because He knows so much more than we do, a closed door or a no is sometimes the answer and it is the correct answer.*

Lesson Learned

- Our value is not in what we have but rather in who has us. If the one who has us is the G-d of Abraham, Isaac and Jacob, the creator of heaven and earth and in His son Jesus, then we are invaluable and our worth is unshakable.

- The fear of losing everything is worse than losing everything. When you no longer hold onto things with a closed fist, you are in a place where things can be placed into your hands.

- Sometimes it is not what we do that is right or wrong, but why we do something. Always check your motives and make sure pride is not the motivating factor.

Chapter Eight
Success is Born

At this point I had gone three years without an income. Left with
no other choice, I had to file bankruptcy.

The Stein Group Inc.

All my efforts exhausted. I was out on my back deck telling G-d
things He already knew. I reminded Him He created man with
three purposes, according to the book, "Raising a Modern Day
Knight," by Robert Lewis. The three purposes are to have a G-d
to serve, a woman to love, and a work to do. I had my G-d I
served, and a woman to love, I just needed the work to do. For
the last two years, everything I touched seemed to fail.

I asked what I was supposed to do about this situation when
I heard, "you love finding money and originating loans—start a
mortgage brokerage for commercial loans."

I immediately walked in the house, sat at my desk with a legal
sized pad and began writing. Just like with the deli, my mind was
racing; I was flooded with thoughts, pen and paper in hand. This
time however, instead of writing down things I needed to do or

find out how to do, I made two lists. The first list was the names of lenders that I had relationships with. The second list was of developers and builders that I had come to know over the years.

I immediately began calling both. I had been out of the lending business for two years and needed to find out the current rates and terms. I needed to know what lenders had an appetite for. Different lenders like doing different loans at different times based on what is currently in their portfolio of loans.

After learning what I needed from the banks, I started calling the people on the second list. If they owned apartments, I inquired as to whether they needed to refinance existing loans, if they needed to go from a construction loan to a permanent loan, or if they were looking for construction dollars to build another project. I called commercial real estate investors to see if they were looking to purchase additional properties. If they were developers, I checked to see if they had sites they didn't have financing in place for yet and so on. The response was positive and I was on my way.

I asked my wife what I should name the company and she came up with the name, The Stein Group. She said it gave the company a feeling of solidity, firm-like, and not a one-man show.

I made another list. This time I wrote goals I wanted to achieve by the end of the year. The list may sound funny to you, but it was very real and, at the time I wrote it, it took a lot of faith to believe.

1. Have the money to have business cards made

2. Have the money to order business letter head

3. Have the money to get legally bonded

4. Have the money to install a separate phone and fax line for the company at the house

5. Have the money to incorporate

Allow me to regress for just a second. When I read "Pizza Tiger," the story of Domino's Pizza by Tom Monaghan, I felt worn out at the end. Tom had gone through so many failures and hostile take over's before he sold Domino's for one billion dollars, that I felt nauseous riding the roller coaster of success and failure with him. In my fears of exhausting the reader, I find myself hesitant to continue listing my failures. With caution, I tell you the Stein Group only closed one loan the entire year.

With each loan I worked on, something completely random and out of the blue occurred. I spent days putting together a comprehensive loan submission package for a local businessman with many apartments and a loan coming due that needed to be refinanced. On my way to the bank, literally while driving to meet with the lender, my phone rang. My client informed me he just sold a piece of land and would pay off the loan rather than refinance it.

Another time I had secured a loan for a man who was going to build a strip shopping center. I had his loan approved; it was scheduled to close on a Thursday. The call came on Tuesday— he had cold feet and decided not to build it.

Another loan was approved when, on a whim, the out-of-state lender came to the town where the project would be developed. He did not feel the town was up and coming and declined the loan. The town happened to be the third fastest growing town in the entire state. I provided the data but it didn't change his mind. I even had a client die. I could go on, but you get the point. For one solid year, only one loan closed.

At this point I had gone three years without an income. Left with no other choice, I had to file bankruptcy. This was one of the worst days of my life. I felt so good about the testimony I had with my first business failure and how I didn't go bankrupt but paid back everyone I owed. Now, all these years later, I'm declaring bankruptcy after all the lessons, all the personal growth, and all the successful achievements under my belt as VP of a major company.

I filed in September of 2001. Then a very strange thing happened, my loans began to close. All the loans that had previously fallen apart began to close. The apartments in the one town they said was not in a growth area, I found another lender and they closed. The guy with cold feet sent his buyer to me and I did the loan for him to build the center. The man who died, rose from the dead, just kidding. One by one, I began to close loans.

Why, for the first time in three years I began making money the same month I declared bankruptcy is beyond me. I would not have planned it that way, but that is how it happened. Like I've stated before, sometimes up is the only alternative when you hit bottom. I couldn't make the loans start happening, but I did understand how to handle the wealth they would bring as a result of all I went through.

By the end of the year I closed just shy of $10,000,000 in loans, made $70,000 and accomplished everything on my list, including turning The Stein Group into The Stein Group Inc.

The next year I did $13,000,000 in loans, then $30,000,000 the following year. By 2007 I was up to $51,000,000 in loans annually.

In the last 20 years I have secured well over half a billion dollars in loans.

I obeyed what the Lord told me for a solid year when there was no other reason to continue. I was told once that when G-d is silent, just keep doing the last thing you believe you heard him say.

The Stein Group Inc. became a successful commercial mortgage brokerage and remains so, more than a decade later.

Lessons Learned

- Winston Churchill, "Never give in, never, never, never…except to convictions of honor and good sense."

- Keep doing the last thing you felt you were supposed to do until you feel a different direction. Stay the course.

- In everything we endure, in all the circumstances of life, there is purpose and destiny. Trust. The more you understand how much the Lord loves you, the easier it is to trust His plan for your life.

Chapter Nine
Defining Moment #4

"The closer you get to your (deadline), the larger the giant. The larger the giant, the more glory I receive for slaying it. Don't panic. Sit back and watch the salvation of your G-d."

It took a year for the bankruptcy to be discharged and, once again, I had the favor of the Lord, as well as the banking community. That same month the discharge occurred, we were able to purchase a house.

We found a beautiful three-bedroom, two-bath log home on three acres of land. Due to the size of our family, my mother-in-law living with us, and the fact that I ran The Stein Group from our house, we knew we would need to build an addition.

I applied for a loan for the purchase and enough money to convert the house into a five-bedroom, three-bathroom house with a loft, a larger dining room and an office.

I was approved, but since the bankruptcy was so recent, the lender wanted me to come up with a large down payment.

The short story below is the way that I *thought* the money for the down payment would be provided.

I had an appointment in a town where I had lived some years back. After the appointment I asked the Lord if there was anything he wanted me to do before I left. Immediately, a friend came to mind. He was a business owner and I felt I should encourage him. We met at a local sub shop for a sandwich and, while there, I came across a man with whom I had done business in the past, but hadn't seen in a while. He was actually a guy who used to own the landscaping company we used on several of our apartment communities. He went on to become a successful businessman, owning a large portfolio of rental houses and other commercial properties.

As it turns out, he was getting ready to buy a grocery anchored shopping center. After some inquiry, I informed him I could secure his financing at much better rates. I walked away having a lead which led to a several million dollar loan.

If I had not made myself available for purposes outside of myself, I never would have met up with him at that sub shop and would have never secured that loan. The favor of G-d that I depend on so much is a result of walking in His plan, not my own.

This situation would prove to be a defining moment in my life, but not in the way you would imagine.

Extremely Important Paradigm Shift

If you can get this, and I mean really get what I am about to share with you, it will change your life forever.

In the past, I believed the Lord was my source and He used my job as the provision, which isn't a bad way to think. When the dust settles, you know G-d is ultimately your source and not your job. You trust in him, not your job. You are thankful to him, not your job.

After Crash # 2, the deli crash, I realized G-d was not merely my source; I realized G-d was actually the provision as well. The fact that I had gone three years with no income brought me to realize G-d did not need a job or a business to provide for me. He could use anything He wanted. During that time he provided in ways I would not have imagined. One time He used insurance money from someone using the side of our car to stop when their breaks went out. Another time He used a smart accountant who went back to a time when we were paying a lot of money in taxes and did a loss carry forward for us. I could go on.

In spite of all these lessons, I was about to experience a deeper revelation of this whole *G-d is the source G-d is the provision* thing.

As a result of securing the loan for the gentleman I met up with again in the sub shop, I believed I would have the down payment for the log home we were getting ready to purchase. I saw this as the Lord providing the needed funds. My focus was on the loan, not the Lord, even though I knew it was the Lord who provided the loan.

As we were preparing to close the loan, a very disturbing fact surfaced. The seller of the shopping mall was unaware the current loan had a lockout period. This is a specified period of time that a loan cannot be paid off, even with a pre-payment penalty. The most common reason for such a clause is to insure the investors that the loan will not be pre-paid before they have had a chance to make a certain amount on their investment.

The loan can be assumed by another borrower but not paid off. This meant I had another 90 days of work ahead of me before I would be able to close the loan. Worse yet, it meant I would not close his loan in time and, therefore, did not have the money I needed to buy my home.

I decided not to say anything to anyone, only my wife. We didn't tell the realtor, the seller, the attorney, or even the lender. We just began to pray.

Just like we did over a decade earlier that rainy day at the office building, we went to that log home and prayed. We went to the house everyday and prayed.

I kept a journal during that time and wrote down what I believed the Lord was saying to me. The most significant entry came just a week before the closing date.

> "The closer you get to your date, the larger the
> giant. The larger the giant, the more glory I re-
> ceive for slaying it. Don't panic. Sit back and
> watch the salvation of your G-d."

After exhausting all my efforts to find the money, I finally looked to the Lord. Not to how He could or would provide, just to Him. I flushed everything out of my mind and focused on Him and Him alone, the person of Jesus.

In the beginning I would have trusted in my business or I would have trusted in all the other ways G-d could have provided. *This time, I was trusting only in the <u>person</u> of Jesus.* This trust meant depending on Him, regardless of the outcome. I believed in my heart it was the next step for my family; G-d would provide. I gave complete control to Him.

We were scheduled to close on the house Wednesday morning at 10:00am. Through a series of events, and people I never would have expected, the money was in our hands by Tuesday at 11:00PM, the night before. We had the money.

Complete trust in G-d, the provider, is the greatest lesson I have learned in life for business and finances. But it didn't come natural, and for quite some time.

I constantly calculate numbers in my head. I do it for fun, calculating random facts and figures. I would always calculate how many loans I was working on, how much they were for and how much I would earn when they closed. I would think about when they were scheduled to close and what my expenses were for the month, when they would be due and how that all correlated in order to make sure the bills were paid on time.

In order to trust G-d as your provider, you cannot dwell on something else as your provision. *It took a long time to train myself* to stop the mental calculations once the revelation came that the closings didn't pay the bills, the person of Jesus paid the bills.

When I say a long time, I mean years. It took years until it was natural to trust in the person of Jesus. At the first sign of a financial dilemma, I found myself back at my internal calculator, punching in the numbers. Each time required a conscious effort to stop crunching the numbers and trust.

If you do something long enough, it becomes habit. After literally years, I retrained my thought patterns to line up with the spiritual truth that G-d is my provision. I cannot express the freedom this brought. My dependency was no longer in an institution or a monetary unit. Do you realize the US Dollar is not even backed by gold anymore? Do you really want to limit the creator of the universe to a piece of paper?

You will often lose faith if you pre-determine how your provision will come, by what means and in what timing. But if you take your trust off of the how, when and where and simply trust in the person of Jesus to supply your needs, He comes through every time.

This is the secret to surviving the unprecedented economic times that are only getting more uncertain. What we have always known will not be reliable. The way we have always done things will not be the way we do them anymore.

Look at how all our crutches have been kicked out from under us in recent years. Many who were rich have lost everything. Reliable jobs have disappeared, 401Ks and pension plans have been reduced to pennies on the dollar. Only Jesus has remained the same. Only the person of Jesus has proven to be the best investment. Why? Because only He makes the claim that He will provide all our needs according to His riches in glory by Messiah Jesus in Philippians 4:19. Because only He makes the claim that He will never change. Economies change, governments change, people change; G-d does not change.

If you don't get anything else out of reading this book, remember that looking to the person of Jesus, not your job, your business, your investments, your check book, or anything else, just the person of Jesus is the way to survive an uncertain economy.

Lessons Learned

- Walking in the favor of G-d comes from walking according to His plan for your life, not your plan for your life.

- The closer you get to your crisis, the larger the giant. The larger the giant, the more glory the Lord gets for slaying it.

- A secret to surviving in these economic times is to look solely to the person of Jesus and not on the things that He may or may not use to meet your need.

- Train your mind to automatically look to the person of Jesus only, in every situation. I truly believe this will be the only way to survive the days we live in and the days to come.

Chapter Ten
Another Successful Business is Born

The economic future is growing increasingly uncertain. Recent years have driven the point home. We cannot trust in what we have known, we must trust in the One who knows.

Real Estate Investments

Before Stein Bagel & Deli, I had been riding a wave of success that lasted 10 years. I felt I couldn't do anything wrong—the wave couldn't crash.

After it did, and then crashed again with the attempt to build apartments, and then crashed again with no loans closing in the first year of The Stein Group, I became very gun shy about trying anything new—much less anything risky.

Then I came across the book, "Rich Dad Poor Dad," by Robert T Kiyosaki. My entrepreneurial spirit came alive again. Everything he was saying made so much sense. I was inspired by the concept he put forth that **a profession that makes money**

deal by deal should only serve for reinvestment in a profession yielding residual income. This is the very lesson I taught my children through Bubble Belly Gumballs. Here I am, all these years later, not heeding the concepts I always knew.

Since The Stein Group, Inc. was doing well; I didn't feel the pressure to pursue alternate means of income. My problem wasn't that I needed to work more, but that I needed to work in such a way that my income would be residual. In this way, I would not just be building immediate wealth; I would invest into a more secure, stable future for my family and me.

In his book, "Multiple Streams of Income," Robert G. Allen claims that people should have at least 10 different streams of income. I had a 401K, an IRA, the mortgage brokerage and I did some financial counseling; but I didn't have any real source of residual income. If any of my sources of income were to dry up, I had nothing to fall back on.

The obvious answer was something I knew better than anything else—real estate. The only problem, I was afraid. I was afraid I would fail and lose everything all over again. I was afraid I didn't have it in me anymore, and if I ventured outside the safety of The Stein Group, I would fall on my face.

In his book, "Doing Business G-d's Way!" Dennis Peacock explains the connection between the economical principle of ROI (return on investment) and the biblical principle of sowing and reaping. He points out G-d's obvious interest in His people trusting Him with their investments. The realization that G-d even cares about how we invest our resources gave me the confidence I needed to venture out once again.

Although I had made the decision to purchase real estate, I wasn't the old Dean who jumped feet first into the fire. I surprised even myself in how methodically I entered the arena.

The Lord spoke to me and said, "**Waiting is when you hold off until I say go. Hesitating is holding off once I have already said go.**" I wanted to wait, not hesitate, so I began researching the markets.

I considered apartments, rental houses, and commercial real estate. In part two of this book I will go into the pros and cons of each. I decided to go with individual rental houses. Then I began to pray.

I spent an entire year looking and praying for the right opportunity. One day, a bank I did business with called me. They had a portfolio of 15 houses going into foreclosure. This was in 2004, before the banks REO (Real Estate Owned) portfolios were bursting at the seams as they became after the 2008 crisis.

I looked at the houses and then used the "14 steps to buying real estate" found in "Multi-Family Millions" by David Lindahl. I also used the "Property Selection Grid" found in "Multiple Streams of Income," by Robert G. Allen. The formulas found in these books rate the properties from poor to excellent on such areas as seller's motivation and flexibility, location, available financing, price points and property condition. By assessing a point value to each factor, the total score helps you determine if the investment is right for you.

Steinway Investments LLC

I started by creating an LLC. An LLC has all the protection of a corporation and all the tax advantages of a partnership. It is the best vehicle for moving around real estate. I named the company Steinway Investments because the Steinway piano is a name synonymous with quality and success. In addition, being the sole owner of the company, I had the liberty of conducting all business the "Stein way."

I structured the loan to purchase the 15 properties with no money down and actually put $10,000 cash in my pocket at closing.

The houses had not been kept up and they were either vacant or the tenants were months behind in their rent.

I did the small amount of cosmetic work that was needed, gave the tenants a chance to bring their rents current and issued eviction notices to those who did not keep their word.

As a believer in Messiah, the idea of eviction is something I had to confront from an ethical standpoint. During my time overseeing over 6,000 apartments, I developed a philosophy about evictions. The premise was based on the fact that everybody falls on hard times and everyone deserves a chance. As a result, I would ask those behind in their rent to give a reason for the delinquency. As long as the story seemed legitimate, I asked them how much they could pay and when they could pay it. Sometimes it took several months to get them back on track, but as long as they did what they said, when then said they would do it, I instructed the managers to work with them.

I also understood that circumstances change. If a person said they would be in each Friday with an extra $100 and they called on Thursday to say they could only come in with $75, we still worked with them.

What I did not have grace for was when people did not do what they said they would do, or did not communicate with me. I believe everyone deserves grace and second chances extended for as long as they are willing to make the effort to recover. But if my tenants neglected the chance to make things right, I had no choice but to issue the eviction.

I believe this is the proper way to handle landlord/tenant situations. If, as a result of reading this book, you purchase rental property, always keep in mind that most people will make things right if you give them the opportunity; they just need help now and then. As long as they are honest, work with them. If they are not honest, and this may sound cruel, you should evict them. Unfortunately, some people are going to use you for as long as you allow them to. Using this same philosophy, I ended up evicting most of the tenants that were months behind in their rent. Those that caught up proved to be great tenants.

You Take the Good with the Bad

Four of the houses were a thorn in my side. They were in a high-crime neighborhood and I would never have purchased them, but it was part of the deal to get the other 11 houses I did want. The problem with rental property in high-crime neighborhoods is that it is difficult to get tenants who want to live there.

I asked the Lord what I should do. I knew the houses were a burden to me, and I didn't want them to be a burden to someone else, so how was I going to sell them? The houses were broken into when they were vacant, tenants were not paying rent when they were occupied and there was a drainage problem I inherited when I bought them.

In the last chapter, I mentioned that if you are going to survive in this economy, you have to look to the person of Jesus to meet your needs. The same is true for this next lesson. If you are going to survive in this economy, you must learn to live your life under the voice of the Lord. Creative ideas come from Him, He is the beginning of wisdom, He knows the future and He can and will guide you if you ask Him.

The economic future is growing increasingly uncertain. Recent years have driven the point home. We cannot trust in what we have known, we must trust in the One who knows.

I did what I knew to do; I prayed. Immediately, I remembered one of my tenants in that neighborhood had a brother in the NBA. I asked if her brother would like to buy all four houses. It turned out her brother was not interested, but her pastor was. He was the minister at the church across the street and had an outreach to Vietnam Veterans and abused woman.

It was a perfect fit. Not only would the houses no longer be a burden to me, they would even be a blessing to him. I fixed the drainage problem so he would not have to deal with it down the road. I owner financed the properties for him for one year. He then secured his own loan. Everybody won. Win-win situations are the only way to do business.

With the four houses sold, I was down to 11 rental properties. I prayed that the Lord would lead me to more deals. A few months later, while sitting in an attorney's office waiting to close a loan, I struck up a conversation with someone else who was waiting to close the sale of a house he had built.

He built a sub-division earlier in the year and all but two houses sold. He said he would love to sell the other two before the end of the year. After visiting the houses, I made him an offer that was a win for me, and since I was offering to buy both houses, it was a win for him as well.

Another time, I found a house for sale in an estate. It was only two years old, but the woman who bought it was moved to a nursing home and her children were selling it. This created a scenario where the sellers were motivated due to the property costs they inherited (Taxes, insurance, mortgages, etc.)

I told the sellers' realtor what I could afford, which was a few thousand dollars shy of what she believed they would accept. I proposed that I forgo getting a buyer's agent, who would take 3% of her 6% commission, if she would only charge the sellers a 4% commission. In this scenario, I win since I get the house for the amount I can afford. The sellers win by making the sale and still realizing the same amount of cash. The realtor wins by finishing with a 4% commission instead of 3%. Did I mention I love win-win situations?

I was having lunch with a man who built a house and now could not sell it in a post 2008 housing crisis economy. He was having trouble making the interest payment each month and had also put $30,000 of his own money into building the house. I recommended he rent the house to offset the interest payments but he did not feel comfortable as a landlord. The truth is, it's not for everyone.

I had a plan. I would buy his house for the existing loan amount, plus $10,000. He would carry the difference as a second mortgage. In this way, he would no longer have the monthly payment and would put $10,000 in his pocket. With this purchase price, I was able to price the house at a competitive rental rate, make a small profit each month, and close on it with no money out of pocket as a result of him carrying the second. I would rent the house for one year, or until the market turned around. When I sold it, he would get the first $20,000 and we would split the profit 50-50. At the risk of sounding redundant, have I said I love win-win situations?

With the purchase of these homes, it was official. Not only did I have the Stein Group Inc., a successful business financing other people's real estate, Steinway Investments LLC was also a successful company. To date, I have 21 investment properties. With the opportunities that a post 2008 housing economy offers, I look forward to growing that company even more.

I believe this is the time to purchase rental property. The housing market had been artificially inflated and the values of homes had been unreasonably high in many markets. This is not the case anymore. Just like a pendulum swings far left and then far right, I believe the overinflated housing market is now underinflated. Values may never return to the place they once were, but they will certainly go higher than they are now.

Most builders and their lenders are motivated sellers. Not only can deals be found in looking at foreclosures, but, as I mentioned earlier, builders want to sell just to get out of the monthly interest payments. At the same time, many lenders are making what is called a short sale. That is where they agree to let the builder sell the house for less than the loan just to get it off their books. This means you buy the house for less than it cost to build it.

Add all this to the historically low interest rates, and the perfect scenario arises to purchase rental property of any type. From an investment standpoint, this is truly one way to, not only survive, but to thrive in this post 2008 economy.

Every coin has two sides and before making any business decision, you need to look at both.

With the housing market being in such disarray, some builders are renting their own homes rather than selling them at a loss. Over time, this could cause a glut in the market of rental houses. Another factor to consider is unemployment. When unemployment is high, there might be fewer potential renters than there once was.

Overall, moving forward with calculated steps, there is a lot of opportunity out there.

Part two of this book we will get into why rental real estate is such a good investment. We will discuss the four ways this approach can yield returns. Take the time to review the information and decide if this type of investment is right for you.

We will also look at commercial real estate. You don't hear as much about commercial real estate in the news but the same scenario exists.

Lessons Learned

- The principle of investing and return is the biblical principle of sowing and reaping.

- Waiting is holding off until G-d says go. Hesitating is holding off after G-d says go.

- A secret to surviving in these economic times is learning to live your life under the voice of the Lord. Only He knows the future and can successfully navigate you through this financial land mine.

- Win–win situations are the only way to do business.

- A way to thrive in this economic climate is to capitalize on the low values, and historically low interest rates, while helping others out at the same time.

Chapter Eleven

Crash # 3 The Economy

The banking industry didn't change, but my ability to prosper within that broken industry did change.

Crash #3- The Economy

The first crash I experienced (HIS Co.), was entirely my fault. I didn't know what I was doing and I did it with all my might. The second crash (Stein Bagel & Deli) happened in spite of crossing every T and dotting every I. This crash served to strip me of everything I trusted and bring me to acknowledge G-d as the true provider.

This third crash, however, was a horse of a different color. Everybody experienced it. This wasn't my personal crash or anything I could have controlled; essentially the whole world's economy suffered the devastating results of the 2008-housing crisis.

Before the crash, my job was to make successful people more successful. During this crash, my job evolved into helping people hold on to what they had and not lose everything.

Developers with large tracks of land had their builders walk out on them at the last minute, leaving them with fully drawn loans and no sales to pay off the debt or income to pay even just the monthly interest payments.

Newly built houses were now standing empty with no potential buyers. Some of the homes in my area cost 4 and 5 million dollars to build. The homebuilder would have to pay $20,000 a month for each unsold house just to cover the interest on the loans.

Think about the ripple effect. Not only were builders not making an income, they were having an enormous amount of debt to cover each month.

Real Estate investors, in the middle of construction on an office building or shopping center, all of a sudden couldn't lease or sell their space. They may have had pre-sold units or signed leases with tenants poised to take possession, but these prospective buyers and tenants had the rug pulled out from under them as well.

Speculators who purchased large tracts of land to sell to developers were losing the land because they couldn't sell the property.

In the beginning of the economic crisis, I spent much of my time working out deals between lenders and borrowers to help the borrower not lose the property and the lender not get it back.

Here we are over five years later and I am still negotiating these work-outs. Today, lenders are much more reasonable with their expectations. This results in many more opportunities to thrive in today's economy.

Lesson Learned

By the time this crash occurred, I had already learned the very important lesson of trusting in the person of Jesus.

I went from October of 2008 to March of 2009 without closing a single loan. The banks didn't dare lend a thing. I had plenty of clients and plenty of work to do, just nothing I could close. And since I only charge for a completed, closed loan, I had no income.

It was then, in March that I kept hearing the same message preached form several different places. The messages was simple—contend *for what is yours. The enemy of goodness wants the people of G-d to participate in this crash, but G-d is not of the same mind. Fight for what is yours.*

I began doing just that, in prayer, every morning. I declared what G-d spoke to my heart. I declared that He gave me this business and it was meant to prosper for His glory. Sure enough, things changed as I began to agree with His purposes for my life. **The banking industry didn't change, but my ability to prosper within that broken industry did change**. Starting in April, I began closing loans that others in my business were not getting closed.

I also sought the Lord about the direction I was going. I asked Him if, after over 20 years in this business, it was time to get out. The great thing about totally trusting in the Lord is that you receive counsel from the one who knows the future.

As a result of these prayers I received two areas of direction.

The first came one day when I went outside to walk around my neighborhood. We live on a peninsula, so the entire neighborhood is surrounded by water. I love to walk and pray and look at the lake. Just before leaving the driveway I cried out to the Lord and said, "You have to get me out of this funk." I don't normally use the word "funk" so it stood out to me when I said it. Later that evening, I had a young couple to come over for financial counseling. After helping them to develop a budget and start on a road to debt reduction, the husband said to me, "Thanks Dean for getting us out of our financial funk." I thought, that's twice in one day, there must be something to this.

That's when it hit me that so many were going through the same thing as a result of this economy that has fallen off a cliff. I should put on seminars to help people through it. I named them "Freedom From Financial Funk" and began teaching groups how to navigate through these unprecedented times.

This book that you are reading now is in part a by-product of those seminars. Especially Part 11.

The second result of praying for direction came when I felt a strong impression that I should get my real estate license. That's right; I was going to get my real estate license in a post 2008 housing crisis economy. In the natural, that seems like the most irrational next move imaginable. Get your real estate license in a time when nothing is selling? However, what I understood is that I could go to the very same banks I used to take clients to for borrowing money, and help them get rid of the properties they were getting back from borrowers.

Later that very day, I spoke with two different people (not one; two) who asked if I had a real estate license. I called a school, signed up, took the class, took the test and got my license.

I connected with a commercial real-estate firm I had known for over 20 years. They worked closely with banks and only in commercial real estate, not residential.

In the first year, I sold several commercial buildings that were given to me to sell from lenders who had taken them back in a "deed in lieu of foreclosure" (a topic we will cover in Part II). By the second year, I had made 5 times what I did in the first year.

Banks were in denial in 2008 and even through 2009. They began getting properties back from borrowers, but were trying to sell them at small discounts. Beginning in 2010 and certainly into 2011 and 2012, they realized they would have to start selling these properties at greater discounts.

They also began to offer very favorable financing terms for these properties.

I formed another LLC with a partner and bought several more houses to add to my rental portfolio. The financing terms included 100% of cost, a ten-year fixed rate at 3.99% and a 30-year amortization. These were also bought at a price substantially lower than the current appraised value. A perfect example of not only surviving, but thriving in this post 2008 economy.

Having my real estate license has enabled me to increase my monthly cash flow in other areas as well. I've been able to manage several retail centers for lenders who ended up with the properties and had no way of operating the centers themselves. I've created income by helping clients rent their vacancies and so on.

My greatest increase to date has been that, as a result of working with Metrolina Capital Advisors (MCA), I have been able to pick up clients I would not have had access to otherwise. I am getting these deals financed for clients, which blesses them, the banks, and the company I hung my real estate license with—talk about your win-win-win situations.

And so, a third successful company is born. The Stein Group Inc. secures financing for other companies' commercial real estate. Steinway Investments LLC purchases residential real estate for residual rental income and, now joining forces with MCA, I am working with banks to sell their REO and OREO.

Living in Goshen

When the Jews were in Egypt and judgment came on the Egyptians for refusing to free the enslaved Hebrews, G-d's people did not endure the plagues. They were in Egypt but not part of the judgment.

We as the people of G-d have a purpose to fulfill in an economic downturn. If we refuse to participate in greed and lust, and trusting in the riches of this world, then the shaking of this world economy is not for us. On the other hand, if your heart is in the things of this world and not the creator of this world, then it is time to turn to the Lord of the economy.

Many people have lost or are losing everything they have. The things they have trusted in have failed them. You have a unique opportunity to help them. You can do this by giving to them financially, showing them the way spiritually, and even by entering into win-win business deals with them.

In Conclusion

If we actually evolved from animals, which resulted from this big explosion in the cosmos, and we ended up here on this tiny planet with everything as just a series of random happenings, then there is not really much to motivate us to be all we can and should be. Life really doesn't have a purpose or meaning or eternal consequence.

On the other hand, if we are created with purpose, with a plan for our life, and are being watched over by a loving G-d who created us for greatness, one who guides us along the way so we can reach that greatness, then life is an incredible adventure. We can know there is meaning and purpose for all we go through.

The scriptures say in 3 John 2, "Beloved, I wish above all things that you may prosper and be in health, even as your soul prospers."

As I look back over my life in business, I see a clear picture of a roller coaster. I started down low, went up high, dropped rapidly to the bottom, climbed back to the top, only to do it all again.

What is interesting to see is that, with each failure, I climbed higher. I became more successful after each crash. The crashes were valuable lessons I learned that allowed me to climb higher each time to a new personal and financial plateau.

Each low point in my life developed character in me that could not be learned any other way. It is only through fire that gold and silver are refined. The fire melts away the imperfections, resulting in something of more value than before.

The Lord once spoke to my heart and told me He was not as concerned about my temporal comfort as He was about my eternal destiny.

G-d won't promote you beyond your character; that is what 3 John 2 means.

Joseph spent 15 years enslaved and imprisoned while G-d prepared his character to be second in command in Egypt, the world superpower of his time.

Moses spent 40 years in the desert while G-d prepared his character to lead the children of Israel out of captivity, into their destiny.

Joshua spent 40 years in the wilderness while G-d prepared his character to lead the children of Israel into the Promised Land.

David spent 13 years running from Saul in the desert while G-d prepared his character to be the King of Israel.

In his book, "The Prayer of Jabez," Dr. Bruce Wilkinson teaches on a prayer found in 1 Chronicles 4:9. In that little prayer is the line "Oh that you would bless me indeed and enlarge my territory." Don't you know it hurts having your territory enlarged?

If you are going to have your territory enlarged, then you are first going to have your *capacity* to handle that territory enlarged. G-d is not going to give you enough rope to hang yourself.

Why, so often when people win the lottery, do they end up broke and worse off than before they won, often times within a few short years? It's because they never developed the character to handle the blessing. The blessing became the curse.

Wilkinson goes on to say, "To bless, in the biblical sense, means to ask for or to impart supernatural favor. When we ask for G-d's blessing, we're not asking for more of what we could get for ourselves. We're crying out for the wonderful, unlimited goodness that only G-d has the power to give to us."

You are fearfully and wonderfully made and G-d has a uniquely amazing plan for your life. Believe it, and you can endure the testing that will eventually get you there.

Think of it this way, if you are called to be a doctor or a lawyer, will you not spend 8 years of your life in preparation for the eventual reward? Enough said.

I am not under some false illusion that I have been through all the testing I will ever go through and now all I have to do is ride the wave of success from here on out.

I believe I am called to be more successful than I am right now. That being the case, there is more character that needs to be formed in me to handle the additional riches I am called to steward.

As we come to the close of Part 1 of this book, my hope is that having read the mistakes that I have made in my journey, you will be better prepared to avoid those same pit-falls. At the same time, it is also my desire that by reading the lessons the Lord has taught me, you will have the faith to hear Him for yourself on the road through your own entrepreneurial journey.

Hang on—here we go again to new heights.

Part Two
Let's Get Practical

Chapter Twelve
The Infamous "Joseph Calling"

Wisdom vs. Gold

Proverbs 16:16 "How much better is it to get wisdom than gold! And to get understanding, rather to be chosen than silver!"

Proverbs 8:11 "For wisdom is better than rubies; and all the things that may be desired are not to be compared to it."

What King Solomon (the wisest man who ever lived) is trying to tell us is that, while gold and rubies are very valuable, the wisdom to know what to do with them, the wisdom to know how to hang on to them and how to make them work for you, is actually more valuable than the gold itself.

In Chapter 11 I mentioned how so many people who win the lottery end up losing it all and even declaring bankruptcy because they increase financially beyond their character development. Proverbs 20:21 says, "An inheritance may be gotten hastily at the beginning; but the end thereof shall not be blessed;"

All these scriptures are saying the same thing; riches can be something that either blesses you, or becomes a curse to you.

Having the wisdom to know how to steward those riches will determine which outcome is yours.

This second part of the book is for that purpose. I am not a Solomon, but what I do have to give to you are lessons I have learned over the past 44 years, since I started my first business at 8 years old. I have also learned to hear the voice of the Lord and to follow him in business decisions. Part two of this book is a compilation of the things I have learned. Some of what you will read is what I have learned in my successes, most of what you will read I learned in my failures.

The Joseph Calling

Before we get into the nuts and bolts of the teachings, let me tell you another story. As you know from part one of this book, by the time I was 27 years old I had already sub- contracted a paper route, had a Five and Dime Store business going door-to-door on bicycle, made a killing for a 12 year old in the beef market, and with a partner, started a home improvement company and a small chain of furniture stores.

Business was without a doubt in my blood and I knew that I loved it, but I didn't see it as part of my calling in life. I saw it as something I did to make a living.

One day I was reading about King David in the book of Samuel in the Old Covenant, and I stopped and said, "Lord make me a David." In other words, make me like David. I have always loved King David. He was my childhood hero as a young boy growing up in the Jewish Foundation School on Staten Island.

One of my greatest thrills as an adult has been the many trips I have taken to Israel. I have experienced the thrill of walking through the very water tunnels that King David's men went through to capture Jerusalem 3,000 years ago, and swimming in the actual pools under the waterfalls in En Gedi that he did.

Forgive me, I'm digressing. When I made that statement about wanting to be a David, I didn't expect to hear anything back, but I did. The Lord spoke to me in such a clear and powerful way that I will never forget it. He said, **"I am not going to make you a David, I am going to make you a Joseph."**

I know that in a lot of churches today, that is a common phrase. A Joseph calling, a Joseph anointing, G-d is making you a Joseph. What you have to understand is that this occurred over 20 years ago and I had never heard that phrase before. I actually had no earthly idea what it even meant. I would discover the many facets to its meaning in the years to come.

There are many, many lessons we can learn from Joseph's life, but in a nutshell, Joseph had an anointing for business. He was successful as a slave in Potipher's house, he was successful as a prisoner in Pharaoh's prison, and he was eventually successful as second in command over all Egypt. He saved the seed of Abraham, the Jews, from starvation so that eventually the Messiah could be born. It took me many years to realize that the reason I had always loved the restaurant business and feeding people, was because of this "Joseph calling," after all, that is what Joseph did, he fed the hungry.

The Life Cycle of a Calling

Like any calling, if it is to be fulfilled in your life, there is a natural progression. You hear the call, you embrace and become excited about the call, then you try to make the call come to pass in your own strength, you fail at the call, you question if you really have the call, you come to hate and despise the call, you give up on the call all together, and then the call comes to pass in your life.

Look at Moses; he knew in his heart that he was to be the deliverer of G-d's people. He tried to intervene and take matters into his own hands. He ended up running away and when it was time for him to rise to the occasion; he wanted nothing to do with it. He eventually became the deliverer he was born to be.

I have gone through the cycle. When I went through my 3 years of not being able to make a dime, I despised the very name Joseph. But as the Lord has brought good in my life, just as he delivered Joseph from the pit, I have learned that my Joseph calling is more for others than it is for myself.

The following condensed teachings are a result of this calling in my life. They are the wisdom that is more valuable then gold. I pray they will be a blessing to you and that they will help you walk out your calling to be a Joseph. You see, the very fact that you are reading this book tells me, you are probably called to be a Joseph or Josephine yourself.

The next several chapters will cover a large range of topics. Some of these topics will deal with business, and some will deal with your personal finances. These teachings are both practical and spiritual.

I have actually devoted an entire chapter explaining the way to do business supernaturally. I believe that this one chapter is the key to getting the most out of all the other chapters. I said in Chapter 6 that I don't understand why you would go to a higher power, when you could go straight to the highest power.

While Part One of this book was a story with lessons learned through the telling of my business adventures, this second part is a series of short "bullet point" teachings.

However, before getting into the "practical" teachings, I want to begin with a spiritual teaching.

I learned a long time ago that what I can do in my own strength pales in comparison to what I can do in His strength.

So, as a result, I need to move from this natural realm with all its limitations, into a supernatural realm with no limitation, if I am truly going to thrive in my businesses.

Chapter Thirteen
10 Attitudes For Doing Business Supernaturally

Doing business on a supernatural playing field is more of an attitude than anything else.

It is your motive, more than your action. It is more of *why* you do something, than *what* you do.

The following are the attitudes I work to incorporate in my business practices.

> 1. *My life is not my own, I was bought with a price -*
> 1Corinthians 6:19, 20

With this as the cornerstone of your foundation, everything you do, all that you see will be through a selfless grid. Acknowledging this fact will make it natural to be humble and honest in all your business dealings.

> 2. *I am His workmanship and have been*
> *created for specific good works that*
> *I should walk in* - Ephesians 2:10

Life becomes an adventure when you spend it finding and walking in the "good works" that have been prepared for you. You tend not to get so stressed when things don't work out as you planned when you have this attitude. Knowing that it may not be working out according to your plan, but is in line with a bigger plan makes all the difference.

3. If I trust in the Lord and do not lean on my own understanding and acknowledge Him in all my dealings, He promises to direct my paths
- Proverbs 3:5, 6

I don't need to stress about whether or not He is directing my paths. I only need to trust and not try to figure it all out in my own understanding. If I do my part, He will do His.

4. My life and my career are one because I acknowledge Him in all my dealings.

Proverbs 3:5, 6 and because whatever I do, in word or in deed, I do as unto the Lord, business included– 1Corinthians 10:31, Colossians 3:17

5. The greater includes the lesser; the lesser does not include the greater.

If I concentrate on seeking first the Kingdom of G-d, then I can be assured that the things that I need are going to be added unto me – Matthew 6:33. If, on the other hand, I seek first my needs, then I cannot count on them, (my needs that is), or the Kingdom of G-d as it relates to my life, being taken care of. I seek first the Kingdom by doing number 6.

6. I don't work to make money for myself. I serve the Lord by serving others and getting done what they need.

As a result, I get paid, but my priorities are serving others and not myself. This enables me to make decisions that are not self-serving but rather in the best interest of my clients. I heard Dennis Peacocke say one day that he was not a socialist or a communist, but also not a capitalist. He said a capitalist has for a bottom line, profit. He operates in the Kingdom of G-d economy. That economy has for its bottom line, people. People are entrusted to employers to help them become all they should be. A by-product of this is profit. So profit becomes the by-product, not the goal. Many times in business you come to a cross roads where you can make one of two choices. One choice will be in the best interest of the client but not as advantageous for you. The other choice will benefit you and not necessarily be bad for the client, just not as good. It is in these times when you have an opportunity to act on what you believe in. You choose what is best for the client and let the Lord take care of you. It is a very freeing decision and one with great benefits.

7. All the income from my businesses is the Lord's, not just 10%.

When the Lord gave the talents to the men in Matthew 25:14-30, He made it clear that He was returning and they would have to give an account for what they did with His money. Verse 27 makes it clear that when the Lord gives us His money, it is still His.

Think of it this way. If I came to you with a briefcase full of money and told you that it was yours, chances are you would do good things with that money. You would give some away, buy something nice, and possibly even invest some.

But what if I gave you that same briefcase and told you it was my money and I was leaving it with you to invest for me and am coming back to see how well you do. You would think very differently about what you did with the contents of that briefcase. All we are given is the Lord's. We are merely stewards who will one day give an account.

8. *Since the business is the Lord's and I am only a steward over it, and since it is His money that is made in the business and it is for his purposes, then He is the one who calls the shots.*

He leads me where I should go, shows me how I am to do things, and what things I am to do. When I get a new client, I pray over his deal and ask the Lord what lender to approach. He guides me in the decision. One time when I prayed about where to take a loan, I heard the Lord say a particular bank, but then I heard the name of a banker who did not work at that bank. I took the loan to the bank and was greeted by that banker. He had left the bank he was with and went to work for the bank where the Lord told me to go. I didn't know that, but the Lord did. I closed that loan with no problems.

9. *Personally, the Lord has told me not to market the business.*

I don't put up signs on construction projects when I arrange financing. I do not make cold calls, I do not advertise online or in print. I do not even have my business listed in the phone book. The Lord showed me that if I were to do that I would have to share the glory for the business He sends me, with my own efforts. This is not a carte blanche principle for all businesses, but an example of following the voice of the Lord for each decision

10. *G-d's provision for Gideon was not more men or armor or weapons, it was His Presence.*

The statement, "G-d is not only my source, but also my provision," means that HIS VERY PRESENCE is that provision. The very person of Jesus is that provision. He is not just the provision in the natural things He provides; He is the provision in His very presence, in his very person. Do not look at the deals you are working on as your provision, or even G-d's way of providing your need. Look only at His Presence, the person of Jesus as being all you need.

Philippians 4:19 says that G-d will provide your needs according to His riches in glory by Messiah Jesus. Not that he will provide your needs by your job, or your latest deal, but by Himself. He himself is that provision.

Don't focus your attention on anything else but Him. Not how He will do it, just Him.

You will find that during times when you have exhausted all your resources it is easier to focus only on Him. However, it becomes harder during times when He is providing, because you tend to look at the way of the provision and not the Provider.

I believe the two key points are numbers 5 and 10. Seeking first the Kingdom of G-d and not the business, and then seeing the presence of G-d and not the provision of G-d as being the goal. If we have His presence we have all the provision we need. If we seek the deals as the provision we are not seeking first the Kingdom.

Don't trust in money – Be entrusted with money

Chapter Fourteen
Dos and Don'ts Concerning Money

The following list is simplistic and basic and yet full of truth that, when lived out, will determine your financial success.

As I stated in part one of this book, money is a tool, a means to an end, not an end in itself.

Don't

Don't love it

Don't trust it

Don't depend on it

Don't hoard it

Don't seek to get lots of it

Don't let it be your master

Don't dwell on it

Don't find your value in how much of it you have

Don't borrow it for liabilities

Don't eat your seed (Don't spend all you get, put some aside to reinvest)

Do

Do allow your money to work for you, not just you working for money

Do use money to create value

Do invest money to create value, (purchase & flip, purchase rental property, invest in marketable securities)

Do work to have money to invest, live on the investment income

Do have money to give to those in need and ministries

Do allow G-d to establish your standard of living

Do have multiple streams of income

Do allow profit to be a by-product and Kingdom economics be your goal

Do create residual income

Do realize that the "invest and return" principle is a Biblical concept of sowing and reaping

Let me expound on just a few of these principles.

Don't let money be your master:

In the book, "A Bully Father," author Joan Paterson Kerr, includes a letter from Teddy Roosevelt written to his son Ted in which he comments on his desire to play football in college. He said, "Athletic proficiency is a mighty good servant, and like so many other good servants, a mighty bad master."

Money is a servant, a means to an end and not the end itself. For many, money becomes the master, the end of all things.

The Kingdom of Heaven is the Master, the end of all things. Money is merely a servant, a tool to bring to pass a greater end. This is what I meant in Chapter 3 when I said money is a means to an end that is worthy to be achieved; an end beyond yourself.

Let G-d establish your standard of living:

So many times, as our income grows, so does our standard of living — a bigger house, a nicer car, etc.

Our standard of living should always be based on what we believe the Lord is showing us.

As an example, say I purchase the house I believe the Lord is showing me to buy after seeking His will in the matter. If times get tough, I can have the confidence that He will provide, because I bought the house out of obedience to His leading.

On the other hand, if I just purchase a home because I want it or because I can afford it, when times get tough, I won't have confidence that the Lord will be my glorified slot machine and provide me with all my lust and indulgences according to His riches and glory. Philippians 4:19 (paraphrased).

It very well could be that G-d has increased our income to be able to give even more away to others. The blessing could actually be for others and not us. If we are not our own and believe we have been bought with a price, we can be OK with that.

Don't eat your seed:

This one is so important for those of us in business. It is very easy, especially when times are tight, to take all the money from a job and use it for immediate needs. The problem is that inventory needs to be replenished or there will be nothing left for the next job.

Imagine if a farmer ate all his seed one year and had nothing to plant the following year.

In the area of investments, you may not need to replenish an actual good in order to continue, but growth won't happen unless that seed, or investment, is built upon. Reinvest a portion of your gains.

Don't trust in money - Be entrusted with money

Chapter Fifteen
Financial Principles For Debt, Investing, & Spending

One of the saddest stories in the Bible is in 2 Kings Chapter 4. It's a story of a godly man who left his wife and kids in financial bondage after his death.

Now I know that when you die you can't take it with you. However, if you are the breadwinner in your family and you die first, it is your duty to leave your family as financially sound as possible.

This can be done in two ways. You can leave them so much money that they will never have to worry about anything again or you can make smart choices while you're here so that they can continue on financially without you.

Two great saying:
Plan your Work and Work your Plan.
If you Fail to Plan you Plan to Fail.

Let's look at three areas that should be considered in your financial planning, debt, investing and spending.

Debt

Mortgage

It goes without saying that it is best to have no debt at all. If at all possible, make sure you only have debt on income producing assets. Most people just accept the fact that they will have debt on their house. Some financial advisors actually encourage people to pay off short-term debt with a second mortgage or equity line, pointing out that they can deduct the interest and even lower the interest rate.

I believe that if you have a plan for paying your house off and work that plan, then eventually you will live in your home debt free. You can weather storms much better if you don't have a mortgage to pay each month. You can retire needing much less income if you don't have the expense of a mortgage, a perfect example of not needing as much money by reducing your expenses.

There are several different ways to pay off a mortgage early. Paying twice a month will decrease the amount of interest paid each month and therefore increase the amount of principle reduced each month.

Reducing the amortization on your loan from 30 years to 15 will of course cut in half the amount of years it will take you to pay off your mortgage. I personally believe that it is best to keep your amortization at 30 years. Doing this allows you to pay the same amount as if you had a 15 year am, but also allows you to pay at the 30-year rate during months when you just don't have the extra.

Credit Cards

If you have credit cards, make sure you only charge what you can pay off that month. The first time you don't pay it off, tear them up.

The Snowball Effect:

If you already have debt, begin by paying off the smallest balance. Then, when that debt is paid off, begin applying the money that you made that payment with to the next one, and so forth. By applying all that extra principle to the debt, you will be debt free in a much faster time than anticipated. This approach is called the snowball effect.

Again, financial advisors differ in their advice on this subject. Some say it is better to take the debt with the highest interest and pay it off first. I am a strong believer in setting goals and being motivated by the results of short-term goals. That is why I recommend paying off the debt with the smallest balances first. We will discuss goals more extensively in Chapter 17.

If you have four credit cards to pay off and in six or seven months that is down to three and then two, you get excited about seeing results. You have planned your work and your plan is working. This motivates you to keep going.

On the other hand, if you chose a credit card with a really high balance and a year later that card is lower but you still have four cards to pay off, you can get frustrated and feel defeated. The power of achieved success is incredibly powerful in achieving your bigger-picture goals.

Buying a car:

If you must buy a car with credit, make sure you wait until you have enough down payment to always keep the value of your car greater than the debt.

So many times when counseling couples, I hear that if they just didn't have their car payment, they could meet their monthly obligations. Problem is, they owe more on their car than it is worth and, therefore, cannot sell it to get rid of the payment.

Most of the time, doing one of three things can avert this crisis.

* Buy a car you can afford for cash, even if it means that you may have to put off that dream car for a couple more years.

* If you have to get a loan, put down enough on the car to always stay ahead of the depreciation. This way, your car will always be worth more than what you owe on it.

* Opt for a shorter-term loan. Today so many lenders allow you to take 6 years to pay off your car. A vehicle is worth just a little over half of what you paid for it in just two years. Add the cost of the car and the interest they charge over six years to the depreciating value and you usually end up upside-down within one-to-two years.

As I said, new cars depreciate the second they are driven off the lot. Cars lose the lion share of their value in the first two years. If you purchase a two-year-old car, chances are they will still have several years of warranty left and cost almost half of what they were new.

This is usually the best way to purchase a car. In Chapter 7, I mentioned that we had to sell our Jaguar. We bought that car new in January of 1999 for $56,000. By August of the same year we were forced to sell it due to "Defining Moment #3" after "Crash #2". We sold our eight-month-old car for only $40,000. That's when I decided never to purchase a new car again. I would let someone else incur the depreciation and I would take advantage of the savings. I purchased my last car when it was just two years old with only 20,400 miles on it and paid less than half of what it cost new.

Trade In:

Notice the first question a car salesman asks you is if you are going to be trading in your vehicle. Many times, they ask this question even before asking what kind of car you are looking for. The reason is because they need to know how much they are willing to discount your desired purchase before offering you a dollar amount on your trade.

In other words, they raise the price, or lesson the discount so that they can make the trade-in look better.

Never go into a dealership with the idea in mind that your will offer your existing car as a trade. Tell them you want to just purchase the car outright. Negotiate your best deal. Then, after seeing what they are willing to offer, go back and ask what kind of a deal they will give you on your trade. This is the only way you can really see what you are getting for your current vehicle. Most times you will see that it is better to sell it yourself, than just give it to the dealer.

Paying the Right Price:

One way of knowing if you are paying a fair price for a used car is to look it up on a pricing web site such as www.Kellybluebook.com

Look at the trade in value first so you can get an idea of what the dealer paid for it. Then look at the Private Party value so you can see what you could purchase a similar car for from an individual. Then compare the Retail Price on the Web Site to what the dealer is asking.

Investing

You can probably tell by now that I am a strong proponent of investing in real estate. However, investing is not limited to this one avenue. Having all your eggs in one basket is never a good idea.

I would encourage you to go beyond this book and not just look at real estate. It just happens to be where I have the most experience, and see an incredible opportunity in today's economy.

When it comes to investing in the market, I have a great friend in the business, Paul Taylor. It is always good to have a friend in the business. You can check him out at www.capitaladvgroup.com. Check him out.

Rich Dad Poor Dad

If there is one book that inspired me more than any other to begin investing in real estate, I would have to say it was "Rich Dad, Poor Dad" by Robert T. Kyioski.

I want to touch on just a few of the principals found in the book and then encourage you to read it for yourself if you haven't already done so.

This is a great book to read to gain wisdom of principals not specifics. Let the Lord guide you by His Holy Spirit on exactly what He would have you to do.

The best advice I can give you is not to hurry to get something going, let it be in the Lord's time. Gain as much knowledge as possible before making any decisions. Speak to people who have failed as much as those who have succeeded. You can learn more from a person who has failed then from those who never have.

I ventured out on two deals within 4 1/2 months of reading Rich Dad Poor Dad. The first was a house I put an offer of $48,000 on and was willing to go to $50,000. The house sold for $52,000, it was valued at $67,000, I should have just offered the asking price of $52,000. Sometimes you can loose sight of the forest for the trees. In an effort to save a few dollars and create a better investment opportunity, I missed out on the opportunity altogether.

The second was a house a bank would have sold me with 100% financing plus the money to finish it. The loan would have been for $130,000 with an interest rate of only 4 ½ %, I didn't do it because I didn't feel I had enough money in the bank if it took longer to rent then I anticipated, and because it would have only been worth about $139,000 when it was finished and that's not enough profit for the risk.

I let another investor buy it and then did the financing for him and made $1,300 on the deal. I then did three more deals for him for a total of over four million dollars in loans. The guy I sold it to did very well.

Bottom line: It took me almost one full year before I made my first investment after being inspired to purchase real estate. To date, I have invested in 25 properties.

The main point I want to emphasize here is that you don't need instant success, or quick gain. This is counter-culture and takes some un-learning, but it will take you far. Remember the lesson on waiting and hesitating. It's better to start slow and confident. Many of you will start with limited resources. You're taking a risk. Make sure you've crossed your T's and dotted your I's. If you fail, you'll know you did your part and gave it your best, but you're probability of success will be much greater, and the reward of your labor will be even sweeter.

In the book, the rich dad made the boys work for no pay so they would be forced to be creative and find other ways to make money besides just working for "the man."

When speaking with young people regarding financial matters, I always try to offer ways to help prevent them from falling into the rat race. It's a lot easier not to fall in at all than it is to get out once you've fallen in.

Kiyosaki brings out several ideas regarding real estate purchases that are creative and helpful when getting started.

One concept he talks about is buying more than you need and working a deal. If you want to purchase a track of land to build on, you may be able to put under contract more land than you need. Then before you are scheduled to close, obtain a contract on the additional land for more than you are paying and use that profit to help pay for your portion of the land with a simultaneous closing. The more land you buy, the cheaper it is per acre. As a result, you create value on the smaller piece you are selling off.

He also brings out the fact that some people buy property in hopes that it will appreciate in value. Although history gave us the impression that we can count on that, recent events have proven that is not always the case. When you buy property, look for the deals that are already worth more than what you are paying for them. Property bought that way pre 2008 is faring much better today, even in the event of the housing crash.

My favorite concept from the book is Kiyosaki talking about when a poor man has one dollar, he spends it and has nothing to show for it. When a middle class man has a dollar he leverages it for things he wants and goes further into debt. But when a rich man has a dollar, he invests it and buys what he wants with the money he makes off the dollar he invested.

Look for these points in your own surroundings. Spend time on how you can take these ideas and make them your own.

Spending

The Generosity Factor

In the book "The Generosity Factor," by Ken Blanchard and S. Truett Cathy, founder of Chic-fil-A, Truett tells the story of two successful businessmen and how they spend their money. **One man uses his wealth to live lavishly and spend his time, talent and treasures on himself. The other man sees his wealth as a tool to be able to do good for others.**

Ephesians 4:28 tells us that the purpose for creating wealth is not to lavish it on ourselves, but rather to give to those in need.

G-d does not want to only be the Lord of our giving; He wants to be Lord of our spending as well.

1John 2 – G-d will only prosper us as far as our character will allow, so we won't fall and think we are something more than we are.

This goes back to what I spoke of earlier of how people who win the lottery often loose it all because of a lack of character. G-d will not give us enough rope to hang ourselves.

In the Event of my Death:

I have a file in my Dropbox. It's called "In the Event of my Death." I have been called on in too many occasions to help those who have been left behind, left to figure out what to do when a loved one dies. Most of the time, they don't know where to even begin. They don't know whom to contact, much less where things are.

I begin this file with what I call "Family of Businesses." This is a list of all the important contacts that my wife will need if I die first.

- Life insurance Agent
- Car and home insurance Agent
- Executer of our Will
- Accountant
- Attorney
- Banks where we have mortgages
- Management Company
- Partners in business
- Mechanic
- Appliance repair men
- Plumber
- Electrician
- HVAC repair
- Etc.

I list all our mortgages, who they are with, what house they are tied to etc.

I keep an updated list of the deals I am working on, and who owes me what.

I have a very detailed map of my desk and file cabinets to explain where important documents are located. Life insurance policies, loan docs, Titles to cars, back up disks for P&L's and Balance Sheets, etc.

Last of all and most importantly, I have a letter to my wife, each of my children, their spouses and each one of my grandchildren. Just a little note to tell them all how much they meant to me.

If we are to be leaders in our life, let us also be good stewards of the blessings in that life, but also good stewards of how we leave those blessings to those after us.

Chapter Sixteen
Time: A Blessing or a Curse

Time is a gift that was created for us. In all honesty, I have a hard time wrapping my mind around it, much like space.

I can somehow imagine how time could continue forever, (even though we are told that time will end, another concept that messes me up), but I can't get my head around how there was a time when time began, just like I can't figure out the infinity, or finiteness of space. If space has an end, then what is beyond it, or how can there be nothing beyond it? I get flustered just thinking about it.

The Bible tells us that G-d created time with a beginning and an end. Eternity is not time forever, but rather the absence of time.

There is much that can be written about this subject. We can talk about how we need to be good stewards of our time, how we will give an account for what we did with our time, etc.

For the purposes of this book and how it relates to our surviving and even thriving in these "times", I want to concentrate on a different area—how the element of time turns a problem into a crisis.

We all have situations that come up in our lives—situations that take us by surprise, unexpected, unannounced, unpredicted. Many times these situations become a crisis.

Truth is, it is eliminating the element of time that takes a situation from being a problem to being a crisis.

Say a poisonous snake bites you. You are one minute from the hospital. Problem. Let's say you are two hours from the nearest hospital. CRISIS.

You have a bill to pay and you don't have the money, the bill is due in one month. Problem. The bill is due tomorrow. CRISIS.

You are out at sea on an oilrig. You spring a leak that can be fixed in a matter of minutes. Problem. You cannot seem to fix the leak and it will take several days, even weeks. CRISIS.

The reality is that most of the time, not all the time, but most, what we think are surprises, unexpected or unpredicted events, are actually not.

They are a result of a lack of planning and not watching over things we should be keeping an eye on. So in truth, we create crises that should really have been just problems, or in some cases, just situations.

In Chapter 17 we will talk about setting goals. By setting short-term goals you are constantly tracking your progress and methodically watching what you are doing. As a result of such planning, very little will take you by surprise.

In Chapter 18 we talk about watching over the very small things in a business so that one day, long before it ever becomes a crisis, you don't turn around and realize you have been throwing away money you could have otherwise enjoyed, or reinvested.

Planning is the key to avoiding the majority of unfortunate and unforeseen events that creep up and take you by surprise–otherwise known as crises.

I had a friend call me up at the first of the month and ask me for money to cover his rent. He had been asking for money from me quite frequently as of late, so I asked him why he didn't have what he needed. He proceeded to complain how bad things always happen to him. He explained how his job was at an upscale car wash/detail shop and that earlier in the month they had been rained out for several days. As a result, he did not have what he needed in rent.

I broke the scenario down for him. A. You knew your rent was going to be due at the first of the month. B. Earlier in the month you knew you would come up short due to the rain days. Then I asked him what he did between the first of the month to the end of the month to prepare for the inevitable day of rent. His answer was he did nothing. You see, this was not a crisis that couldn't have been avoided. It was a situation that needed to be addressed and planned for three weeks earlier.

He had the choice to either make time his asset or let it become his liability.

In 2011, a movie by 20th Century Fox came out called "In Time." The movie had people begin their adult life with a certain amount of minutes. When they bought goods, they had to pay with their minutes and therefore were closer to death. When they worked or sold goods, they would be paid with additional minutes.

This seems far-fetched at first, but with a little contemplation, is it really that far from reality?

We work to make money. This takes our time. If you make minimum wage, then you make $7.25 (At the time of this writing) for every hour of your life that is spent at your job.

Say you want to go out and buy an average watch to track your time and it cost you $30. After tax, you will have to use up about four and a half hours of your life to buy that watch. That's four and a half hours that you can never get back.

Sure is an odd way to think about the time we have on earth, isn't it?

David, whom I mentioned extensively in Part 1 of the book, told me once that he didn't believe in working 60 to 80 hours a week. He knew family and other things were too important to spend all your time on your business. He did say, however, that he believed you should make the most of the time you do spend at work. Make every minute count. Work smarter and harder and be deliberate about what you do and how you do it.

It may be that you are not doing things with your time that you ought to be. On the other hand, it may be you are doing things that just waste time or you are doing them in a way that is not as efficient as it could be.

So, when you are looking at your assets and your liabilities, you have a choice. In which column will you put Time?

Will you allow time to get away from you? Lose track of it? Eliminate it in a situation and therefore create a crisis for yourself causing, it to be a liability to you?

Or will you watch over it, value it, and let it work for you and not against? Remember, time is intended to be an asset. It is up to us to take advantage of that opportunity.

Take some time to think about how you can better prepare yourself against "unforeseen" events. It will be time well spent.

Chapter Seventeen
Setting Goals

I am big on setting goal for a number of reasons. I started off Chapter 15 with two of my favorite sayings:

Plan your work and Work your plan.

If you fail to plan, you plan to fail.

Below I want to illustrate a true story that happened to me when I took my three young sons to Myrtle Beach for a "bachelor weekend."

Our hotel had an Olympic-sized pool. My oldest son Daniel challenged his younger brother, David, to see who could swim the furthest under water.

Daniel took off, but was at a disadvantage since he did not have a defined goal. He obviously could not swim to the other end of an Olympic-size pool underwater, so all he could do was "swim as far as he could."

He ended up going pretty far, and in his mind, he could go no further.

Now it was David's turn, but David had an advantage. His goal was not arbitrary. He wasn't going "as far as he could;" he was looking directly at Daniel's feet.

He had his goal clearly in his sights. As a result, this younger son went further than his older brother.

At this point Daniel said, "Wait a minute, I want to go again." You see, this time Daniel had a clear goal in sight. David's feet.

Off he went, all the way to the spot and past where just minutes earlier he thought he couldn't go.

A perfect example of how we can accomplish so much more, if we set goals and keep them before us.

I prefer short-term goals so that you can stay motivated in being able to mark successes as you go.

One of my family's favorite movies is a film distributed by Touchtone Pictures starring Bill Murray and Richard Dreyfuss, "What About Bob."

In the movie a psychiatrist named Dr. Leo Marvin had just written a book called "Baby Steps." The book helped people tackle big emotional problems by taking one small step at a time.

I believe this is the best way to set goals. How do you eat an elephant? One bite at a time.

If your goals are too lofty, you can easily get discouraged waiting for them to come to pass. On the other hand, if you set small, attainable goals along the way, you will continue to be motivated at every mile marker.

For example, if you want to one day own an apartment building, but you don't have enough of the equity requirement in savings, you have to set goals. Formulate a plan that is within reach that will serve as a stepping-stone in achieving your ultimate, more lofty goal.

Set a goal to purchase a house. Then set a goal to sell the house and buy a duplex. Then set another goal to sell the duplex and purchase a four-plex. Set a goal to sell the four-plex and so on. You get the concept.

It may take you ten years, but at the end of ten years you might just own that apartment building. If you did nothing, in ten years you would have nothing.

Basic tips to goal setting

• Set realistic, attainable goals.

• Set goals in which you can believe.

• Bring others along with you so that they can encourage you when you get weary.

• Set short-term goals along the way to stay motivated as you complete them.

• Commit those goals to the Lord, trust in Him also, and He will bring it to pass. (Psalms 37:5)

Chapter Eighteen
The Size of a Butter Patty

I first introduced "The Size of a Butter Patty" in Chapter 3 as I was sharing that money is only the answer when money is the problem. Most of the time, we throw money at a problem as if it were the ultimate solution to our problems.

As I said before, we do this at every level. In our personal finances, at the local, state, and national levels pertaining to our governments and in our businesses. I spoke extensively about it in Chapter 5 and even referenced it in Chapter 6.

By now, you should realize that I believe this teaching is very significant. The following goes more in-depth with this teaching.

A restaurant will make it or break it based on the size of its butter patty.

This precept is based on the principle of the greater including the lesser but the lesser not including the greater.

If a restaurant is looking so closely at its operations that it actually takes time to consider the size of the butter patty it serves, then it is looking properly and considering everything else.

If the patty turns out to be too big, the excess butter that is not needed is going into the trash on a daily basis. As you can see, the restaurant is not looking at cost control within the business and, as a result, is spending more money for operations than needed.

It may be that a business would be better served to outsource a particular function that they are currently doing in house. In doing so, a company could reduce payroll, thereby reducing all the other expenses associated with that payroll, (taxes, disability, insurance, Workman's Comp. unemployment insurance, etc).

On the other hand, there may be functions that a company currently outsources that could be done more efficiently and cost effective if performed in house.

The deeper you go, the more you uncover. Perhaps there are things your company does because it has always done them. Ask yourself this series of questions regarding all you do.

- Does this benefit my employees

- Does this benefit my company as a whole

- Does this produce income

- Can I do this a better way and produce the same amount of income or more

- What would happen if I stopped doing this? Would there be an adverse effect?

There is not a set answer, the key is to be constantly looking at what and how you are doing business to see if what was the best way in the past is still the best way today.

If the patty is too small, then the restaurant is not looking at customer satisfaction and will lose revenues in the long run.

Just this week I met with a lender with whom I have enjoyed many years of successful loan brokering. This bank provided loans as a community bank as well as facilitating the SBA loans I brought them.

They were just purchased by a larger bank and the first thing they did was to reduce the size of their butter patty so much that they can no longer service their customers in the manner to which they had grown accustom. They even reduced their staff to just one teller. They will ultimately lose customers as a result.

Proverbs 27:23&24 – Be diligent to know the state of your flocks, and look well to your herds, for riches are not forever and does a crown endure to every generation?

Proverbs 6:9-11 - How long will you sleep, oh sluggard? When will you arise out of your sleep? Yet a little sleep, a little slumber, a little folding of the hands to sleep, so shall your poverty come as one that travails and your want as an armed man.

Proverbs 10:4 – He becomes poor that deals with a slack hand: but the hand of the diligent makes one rich.

All these scriptures essentially say the same thing. Don't allow good to be the enemy of best. Don't allow good times to cause you to deal with a slack hand.

Always be looking for ways to spend less and make more. Take your expenses and cost of goods through a stress test on at least an annual basis if not more often.

When I was just 25 years old and in the beginning stages

of opening up our first carpet store, my neighbor who owned a lumber company told me you make half your money selling your product and half the money buying your inventory. This is also applicable to the day-to-day expenses of running your company.

We always seem to go into default and blame our lack on our need to generate more money. The truth is, in many situations, all you need to do is reduce expenses.

Remember, money is only the answer when money is the problem. Take the time to identify problems in your business as it relates to your expenses.

Consider your butter patty in the following areas

- Insurance

- Payroll companies

- Cost of facility (renting vs. owning)

- Cost of vehicles (leasing vs. owning)

- Cost of employees (in house vs. outsourcing)

- Legal

- Accounting

- Banking

- Vendors

The time to be on top of your business is not when times are tough; it is all the time and especially when times are good. Good times tend to lend themselves to waste. When you look for waste in good times, you will be better prepared if times do get tough.

Don't trust in money - Be entrusted with money

Chapter Nineteen
The Pond

I first introduced the concept of "The Pond" in Chapter 4 when I was going through the many lessons and insights my new boss and friend had shared with me.

The pond is so important in terms of stability. If your business is your family's main source of income, or at least a critical component of it, then fluctuations in pay can be extremely troublesome, and leave you in a place where it becomes easy to make poor decisions.

If you have been in a stable job and are looking to venture out on your own, the best advice I can give you as you begin is to be sufficiently capitalized.

Have the money you need to fund your business venture and don't over borrow. Have money to set aside to fill or fund your pond so that you can survive until your business becomes profitable.

Spouses need stability, especially if you are the primary bread winner in your family. If you have any experience or even knowledge of owning your own business then you are keenly aware that at times it is feast and at times it is famine. Don't let this reality cause you to live a financial roller coaster ride in your personal finances.

There needs to be stability and dependability in a paycheck and since owning your own business does not always lend to that; "The Pond" is your best answer.

Let's discuss in greater detail just how the pond works.

You begin by establishing a salary, monthly, bi-weekly, weekly, whatever works for you.

Then, you fill, or fund, your pond with as much capital as you can. When I started the Bagel Deli, I put aside a full year of my personal salary and six months operating capital.

As your business venture begins to make money, you put it all in the pond. At first, you may be taking money out of the pond every week prior to making any contributions to the pond. However, you still take the agreed upon salary on payday.

When times are good, you keep adding to the pond and building the reserve, but not increasing what you take from the business. When times get tough and slow down, or even dry up completely for a time, you keep taking your same salary. You as the owner of the business are dealing with the lack of income, but your family feels the security of a steady paycheck.

Saving money will always result in the size of your pond increasing, never decreasing.

Saving is not spending less, it is putting money away. Spending less is spending less, not saving. Can I put it any other way?

If you think that by purchasing a $500 item for 50% off that you saved $250, you are mistaken. What you did was spend $250. You only paid $250 less than you would have.

If your savings account decreased by $250 for the item, how did you save anything?

Remember, saving is putting money into the pond, and only putting money into the pond.

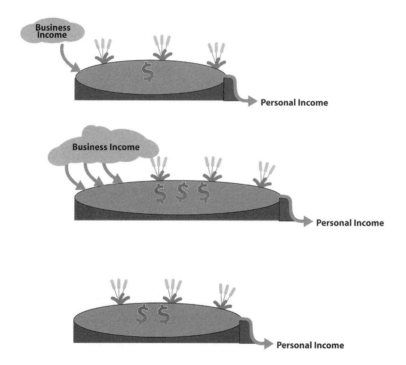

It's crucial to have a checking account for you business from which you pay company expenses, one that is not co-mingled with your personal checking account.

Your company should write a separate check each payday

that is deposited into your personal checking account. I cannot emphasize this principle strong enough. There has to be a separation from your business and your personal finances.

Owning your own business comes with enough challenges in itself. You don't need to add to the stress and pressure by bringing it home with you. Keep your business life and your personal life as separated as you can. The Pond will help you do that.

Chapter Twenty
Let's Talk Real Estate

When we consider all that has happened since 2008 and the reason for the crash in the US economy, our attention is turned to the real estate market as the culprit.

Truth is, the culprit was actually greed. The real estate market was just the collateral damage.

Brokers and lenders were churning out mortgage applications like a well-oiled machine.

Borrowers were ignoring the fact that a variable interest rate loan would eventually increase and that interest only loans would eventually begin to amortize, and when that happened, they would not be able to afford the bigger and more expensive homes they purchased.

Lenders were lending without proper documentation with low doc. and no doc. loans to keep up with the government-led initiative of making sure that everyone could own a house, even if they would never be able to pay for it. It was nothing but pure greed at every level.

As a result of this greed, the real estate market crashed and took with it the thousands of jobs that supported it.

Out of work overnight were builders, plumbers, electricians, roofers, carpenters, masons, surveyors, heating and air contractors, grading contractors, and the list goes on.

Lumberyards began lying off salesmen and store employees for lack of business.

Main Street vendors who sold floor coverings, kitchen cabinets, furniture, window treatments etc. began closing their doors.

As a result of theses stores and businesses closing, retail shops began closing unexpectedly, causing vacancies resulting in the owner of these centers to default on their mortgages.

It was a domino falling ripple effect that came without warning and it hurled us into a recession.

Based on these events, isn't it ridiculous to consider investing in real estate at this time? Wouldn't that be like looking to invest in the stock market in 1930 after the crash of 1929?

The answers to these question are no and yes. No, it is not ridicules and yes it is just like investing in the market in 1930.

In 1929 the stock market was over inflated. People were going to the bank to borrow money at a low interest rate to invest in the market for higher returns. It seemed logical at the time, why not do it?

Problem was, the money they were investing was not really theirs and the stocks they were investing in were artificially inflated due to demand.

When the house of cards came crashing down, people didn't just lose the money they had, they lost money they didn't have.

However, when the dust settled, this over inflated market

had stock prices that were at an all time low. The pendulum that once swung too far one way was now swinging too far in the other direction, thus creating an incredible opportunity.

This is where we find ourselves today. The housing market was over inflated. Prices were out of control. The crash caused values to plummet.

All of a sudden, almost overnight there was a massive amount of inventory with almost no demand. New houses and entire new developments sat looking like ghost towns, and houses that were once occupied sat vacant due to having been foreclosed on.

For the most part, these houses remained on the market. Due to high unemployment, people couldn't purchase the homes and those working found themselves unable to qualify for a home loan based on the new lending guidelines.

During the 2012 election we saw reports saying the housing market is doing better. Truth is, the current market is artificially manipulated.

Lenders have today what is called "Shadow Inventory." This is like a dam that lets just enough product through so as not to flood the market.

If all the houses in foreclosure today were suddenly dumped on the market, it would drive values down again and set us back to 2008 levels.

As a result, the inventory of houses are slowly being put on the market in a deliberate systematic way to keep the supply somewhat level with the demand.

The only good by-product of this crash has been the sustained decrease in interest rates.

With rates at an all time low and real estate at prices lower than we have seen in decades, the same opportunities that existed in 1930 exist today.

So what are we to do with this market?

Chapter Twenty-One

Three Ways Rental Real Estate Makes you Money

There are essentially three ways to make money in real estate. The principles are the same whether you are talking about renting single-family homes, an apartment community, an office or office building, a warehouse, an anchored or un-anchored shopping center or a commercial building.

1. *Monthly residual income from property:*

The first way to make money on rental property is from the monthly rent.

When dealing with single-family or multi-family homes, the tenant usually just pays a monthly rental fee based on an annual renewable lease. You as the landlord should figure out what your annual expenses are and then add at least $150 to $200 per month to that amount. Your basic expenses are your mortgage, insurance, property taxes, landscaping, maintenance and replacement reserves.

One day, if you keep the property long enough, the carpets, hot water heater, HVAC system, roof and appliances will need replacing. You need to set aside a certain amount each month for those inevitable expenses. These expenditures are actually not considered expenses but rather capital improvements that are depreciated over time on your tax returns.

As you can see, there is not a lot of money to be made in residential rental on a monthly basis.

When dealing with commercial property, leases are generally longer, 5 to 10 years with several renewable 5-to-10-year options, having rent increase built in. These leases are usually Triple Net, meaning the tenant pays the rent, taxes and insurance. In most cases CAM (common area maintenance) fees are also included.

When dealing with commercial leases it is always preferential to have what is called a Credit Tenant. Look for a building that was built or is being built for a Family Dollar or a brand name fast food restaurant or a major auto parts store, that type tenant. You can sign long-term leases with these types of tenants and, since they are considered Credit Tenants, your loan terms are more favorable when purchasing the building.

Warehouse space and office space follow the same general rule, although they are usually not credit tenants.

2. *Depreciation:*

The second way to make money on rental real estate is through depreciation.

The income you make on your rental property will be considered either earned income or passive income based on whether or not it is your primary or secondary source of income.

In either scenario, you can depreciate the asset based on a predetermined depreciation schedule. This will lower or even eliminate the amount you pay on the profit you make and in some cases, even lower your tax bracket.

This way of making money is by paying less in taxes and, therefore, putting more in your pocket at the end of the year.

When the property is sold, you will pay capital gains taxes on the difference between what you sell the property for and the basis you have in it. The basis is calculated by the amount you paid and the cost of improvements you added, less the depreciation you took.

3. *Increase in the value of your asset:*

For quite some time, real estate has doubled in value every 10 years. This of course is not the case in our market today. However, one of the biggest advantages to purchasing real estate in this market is that it has nowhere to go but up.

Let me reiterate an important point. You should not purchase real estate with the intent that it will increase in value, but rather make your purchases on real estate that is already worth more than you are paying for it.

The beauty of rental property is that someone else is paying the mortgage for you every month and part of every mortgage payment is reducing the principle amount owed.

On one hand, you have the property increasing in value each and every year. On the other hand, you owe less and less on the property each and every year.

There was a time when you could actually refinance your property and take the difference out and use that tax-free money for whatever you wanted. Those days are long gone but the reality is the principle remains. You build equity in your property each year and will only pay taxes on the increase when you sell.

I don't have a 401K or any other type of retirement program. I will sell half of all my properties when I am ready to retire and use the profit to pay off the other half.

At the end, my plan is to own several debt-free properties and use the rental income for my retirement.

Chapter Twenty-Two
Six Steps to Determine if a Property is a Good Investment

Step One: Location, location, location. In part one I mention that I had once purchased 4 houses in a high crime neighborhood. It didn't matter how nice I fixed up the houses, it was still not desirable due to its location.

If you're dealing with single or multi-family housing you should look for nice clean neighborhoods. Make sure they are in desirable school districts, close to shopping and restaurants and parks.

As I mentioned in Chapter 20, there are excellent bargains to be found in unfinished neighborhoods that have become ghost towns due to the housing crisis. These are usually bank-owned properties that the lender is willing to sell for less than what is owed on it. This is one great area to find real deals. The key though, is to make sure these neighborhoods have not become a haven for the homeless and squatters.

Another important aspect to look at is to make sure they

don't have unfinished amenities such as pools or playgrounds that are left with no way to complete them.

When dealing with commercial buildings, you need to look at the way the city is growing. Are you purchasing something in an up and coming area of town, or the in the area that business is moving away from?

Whether it's residential or commercial, check the vacancy rate in the area. If there is high vacancy, then there is more supply than demand.

Access, parking, zoning restrictions, traffic patterns, these are all essential aspects in determining if a location is not only desirable now, but in the future.

Step Two: Look at the current gross income and determine if there is up-side potential. Many properties are poorly managed and, as a result, the owner is leaving big dollars on the table. Look to see if the rent being received is at the top of the market or not, and if not, why. If it's because of something that you can remedy, then the property is undervalued, which means there is value that you can create. For instance, perhaps you are looking at an apartment community, or a retail center or an office building. The rent you are receiving is much lower than the potential rent due to vacancies. However, when you check the market, you find other properties just like yours in the same area and condition appear to be full. This is a clear indication that poor management is in place and you can increase the monthly cash flow and overall value of the property by bringing in new management.

Step Three: Look at the expenses and see if you could operate the property more efficiently, thereby reducing expenses and again, creating more monthly income. Beyond the immediate gain of added cash flow, you are increasing the value of the asset. Remember in Part One I looked at all the money we were spending on operating our apartments and found ways to reduce expenses? I was able to reduce everything from our paint to our printing to our insurance. Many times, especially if the owner is an absentee owner, properties can be run more efficiently.

Step Four: Gross income is the amount of money you take in. Expenses are the cost it takes to generate the money you brought in. The difference is your NOI (Net Operating Income) before debt service.

A Capitalization Rate, (CAP Rate), is the NOI divided by a certain percentage. In markets where there is more demand than supply, you can see CAP Rates down around 5 or 6 percent. In a soft market like we are in today where there is more supply than demand, CAP Rates can be as high as 11%.

If you have $100,000 a year in NOI with a CAP Rate of 6.5%, from an income approach, your property is worth $1,538,462. With the same income and a market that only warrants an 11% CAP Rate, that same property is only worth $909,091 from an income approach. Understanding your CAP Rate in this example will help you determine the value of an investment. The above example reflects a difference of $629,371 in net worth.

When banks lend on property, they determine the amount

they are willing to lend based on a percentage of the value. This is called the LTV, loan to value.

Appraisers are engaged to determine the value. They do this based on three approaches:

1. The cost approach, which is what they determine it will cost you to rebuild the property.

2. A sales approach, which is what similar property in close proximity to yours sold for within the last 6 months.

3. An income approach.

Many factors besides the market can determine the CAP Rate. These factors include but are not limited to:

- Age of the property

- Location

- Size

- Amenities

Let's use the following example to better explain how this works. Say you are purchasing an anchored retail shopping center in an up and coming part of town. Your risk is relatively low, which means your CAP Rate is also low, causing the price to be higher. If the shopping center you are looking to purchase is in the older part of town and, although all units are full, there isn't an anchor tenant, your risk is higher. The result is that your CAP Rate is also higher, causing the property to be worth less.

With all that said, step four is calculating the value based on the NOI. The key, however, is to base that value on what the current numbers show, not pro-formed numbers.

I can't tell you how many deals I have looked at, not just for myself, but also as a commercial loan broker for others, where the seller was basing the value of the property on the income it could or should generate and not what it was generating. These pro-formed numbers can lead to more problems than it is worth.

They would have 30 or 40% vacancy and run their number based on a 5% vacancy. Problem is that they are trying to cash in on potential value that they did not create. They are telling you to pay for it first and then go out and do the work yourself to create it.

I had a client come to me wanting to purchase a building because it was right next door to one of their other assets and would be a good add to their portfolio.

I asked the seller for their financials and after underwriting the property, I told them that although they were asking $2,500,000, it was only worth about $1,750,000. They argued that I was calculating their value based on the current 40% vacancy and I should be using the markets vacancy rate of less then 10%.

Any lender would calculate the actual, rather than pro-formed numbers, and so would any appraiser. My client would have had to come out of pocket for the difference since the lender would only finance 80% of the value.

I advised my client to pass on the building and they did. A year or so later the crash came and due to the low income the property was generating, they lost it in foreclosure. My client ended up purchasing that very property from the bank for $800,000.

Step Five: Calculate the DCR (Debt Coverage Ratio). This is the ratio between what NOI the property generates and what you pay in debt service. Debt service is your monthly mortgage payment.

The more capital you put into your purchase, the less you borrow. If you can afford to buy for cash, G-d bless you, but most of us can't.

However, work to borrow as little as possible. Most lenders used to look at a 1.10% to 1.20% DCR. Today they don't like to lend on anything without at least a 1.25% DCR.

Calculating the DCR is as simple as taking the NOI and dividing it by your cost of funds. As long as the property is generating at least 25% more than the cost of expenses and your loan, you are pretty safe.

Again, do not calculate this number based on what the property can or should make. Base it on what the property is currently making.

Step Six: Demand Tax Returns. Anyone can give you their internal numbers and make them say what they want them to say.

Without tax returns, you don't really know what the property is making on an annual basis. If they are not willing to show you the tax returns, then they are most likely hiding something. If this happens, your next step is rather simple:

Walk away.

I mention two books in Part One that I highly recommend you read if you plan to further pursue real estate investing. Both have great advice on how to qualify a property. The first book is **"Multi-Family Millions"** by David Lidahl. The second book is **"Multiple Streams of Income"** by Robert G. Allen.

Chapter Twenty-Three
A Few Closing Thoughts on Real Estate

As you look at what type of real estate you might want to invest in, consider each of these alternatives.

Single-family home purchases for rentals will require the least amount of cash to get into. At the same time, they are also easier to sell since they require less money, resulting in a larger number of people who can afford them.

Duplexes and Four-Plexes are a great next step for the same reason as single-family homes.

From there, multi-family apartment communities can give you great residual income. If you can't purchase one yourself, consider finding investors or even partners.

Commercial property usually requires more capital but, as I said earlier, the fact that the leases are sometimes 10 times longer and the tenant pays the taxes and insurance, commercial property is a great investment.

Mini-Storage is also another type of income producing property that should be considered.

What I love about mini-storage, especially if you are going

to build the property your self, is the amount it will cost you to build and operate, in comparison to what you can charge per square foot.

In multi-family apartment projects, you need to carpet or tile the floors, add bathrooms and kitchens, paint and install lighting fixtures, HVAC, electric and plumbing.

In mini-storage, you don't have any of those costs and yet you charge almost as much per square foot to rent out the space.

In addition, the cost to operate the facility is much less. You don't need a full time manager, leasing agent and maintenance person on site. Usually just one person is needed at a time.

All of the scenario's I have shown you are based on purchasing property to be used as rentals. In Chapter Twenty-One I talked about the different ways real estate makes money, and it was all based on purchasing properties and keeping them as rentals. However, another way to thrive in this economy is to purchase property to flip. While this method does not provided for residual income, nor does it allow you to reduce taxes by depreciation, it is still a viable option.

Again, be careful not to purchase property banking on the fact that it will increase in value. Chances are, we may not see values increase significantly for another 5 to 10 years. So purchase property that is already worth more than you are paying for it.

Where to find deals:

There are many different places to find deals in this market. Here are just a few:

- Banks willing to sell property they have taken back in foreclosure.

- Builders whose banks are willing to allow them to sell property in a short sale for less than what is owed on it.

- Banks who have taken property back with deeds in lieu of foreclosure. When a person knows that they are going to be foreclosed upon, they can go to their lender and offer them the deed in lieu of a foreclosure. This saves the bank from all the legal fees and hassles involved in taking a property by force. The borrower can negotiate not having a deficiency judgment as a result of giving the property back.

- Directly from builders who still have inventory. Many times they are willing to sell property for less than they have into it just to get out of paying the monthly mortgage.

- Individuals who know that they are going to be foreclosed upon. Sometimes these people are willing to sell their property for just what is owed on them to save their credit from going bad.

Chapter Twenty-Four
In Conclusion

We can focus on the trouble or focus on the opportunities that the trouble created.

Whenever an industry collapses, we have the tendency to be afraid of that market and run from it when we should be running to it. Truth is; it has nowhere to go but up.

Instead of looking at the real estate market as the **problem** in our economy today, look at it as the **opportunity** in our day; not opportunities to take advantage of others, but opportunities to help others and in the process—create win-win situations.

Talk to your accountant to see what the best vehicle is for you to own real estate in; chances are, your accountant will tell you an LLC.

Next, set up a company and begin to accumulate wealth. Years from now there will be people saying, "I should have invested in real estate after the crash when prices were so good and interest rates were at an all time low. We'll never see those days again."

Closing Remarks

The purpose of this book was to show you ways to Survive and Thrive in this economy.

It's written from an average Joe to average Joes and Josephine's.

One of the reasons I wrote this for you was to eradicate the lie that success is always for other people. Expose the falsehood that success is for people born with a silver spoon in their mouth, people with multiple degrees, tall people, good looking people, anybody but us.

And while the book was not meant to be a "How to" book, I did want to offer practical advice on tried and proven principles, teachings and attitudes that work in your home finances, as well as your business.

I touched on areas of stewardship that brought your focus on the small aspects of your finances, not just the big areas.

I revealed ways to look outside the box and ways to change things within your circumstances when you can't change your circumstances.

I offered you hope that it's OK to fail and to know when to quit but to never give in. Sometimes the failure is because of you and sometimes it's in spite of you, but without risk there is no reward.

I mentioned and recommended many other books for you to read for yourself written by people much smarter than I am. Continue to grow in wisdom and knowledge.

I shared with you the reason for being wealthy and that it lies in what we can do for others more than what it can do for us. How money is a means to an end and not an end within itself.

And most of all, I pointed you to the one who holds our future in the palm of His hand.

Bibliography

Books:

1. Following G-d's Plan for your life: Kenneth Hagin

2. Raising a Modern Day Night: Robert Lewis

3. Pizza Tiger: Tom Monaghan

4. Rich Dad Poor Dad: Robert T. Kiyosaki

5. Multiple Streams of Income: Robert G. Allen

6. Doing Business G-d's way: Dennis Peakcock

7. Multi-Family Millions: David Lindahl

8. The Generosity Factor: Ken Blanchard & Truett Cathy

9. A Bully Father: Joan Patterson Kerr

10. The Prayer of Jabez: Dr. Bruce Wilkinson

11. Baby Steps: Dr. Leo Marvin (Just kidding)

Movies:

1. In Time: 20th Century Fox

2. What About Bob: Touchtone Pictures

Songs:

1. Blinded by Science: Foreigner – Head Games

2. Like a Rolling Stone: Bob Dylan – Hwy 61 Revisited